INVESTIGATING HISTORY

INVADERS — & — SETTLERS

Fiona Goodman and Peter Kent

SIMON & SCHUSTER
EDUCATION

First published in 1991 by
Basil Blackwell Ltd
Reprinted 1991

Reprinted in 1992, 1993 (twice) by
Simon and Schuster Education

Simon & Schuster Education
Campus 400
Maylands Avenue
Hemel Hempstead
Herts HP2 7EZ

British Library Cataloguing in Publication Data
Goodman, Fiona
Invaders and Settlers.
 1. Great Britain, history
 I. Title II. Kent, Peter III. Series 941

ISBN 0–7501–0419–8

Designed by Helen Castle
Illustrated by Peter Kent
Printed in Great Britain by
Redwood Books, Trowbridge

Contents

General introduction

Investigating History is a series of photocopiable resources designed to cover the National Curriculum for History at Key Stage 2. The Programmes of Study are covered through the full range of skills required in the Attainment Targets.

The series offers one book for each History Study Unit. Each book contains a general introduction, an historical introduction, 20 units and a set of Resource sheets. A unit consists of a double-page spread of teacher's notes and a pupils' activity sheet which may be photocopied. Each unit presents stimulating activities which encourage a skills-based investigative approach to History.

Listed below are the Attainment Targets and the outline for the History Core Study Unit 1 – Invaders and settlers: Romans, Anglo-Saxons and Vikings in Britain. Children are required to study one invasion in greater depth. We have chosen the Roman invasion.

Attainment Targets:
AT1 Knowledge and understanding of history
AT2 Interpretations of history
AT3 The use of historical sources

Core Study Unit 1:	Units in book
Invasions and settlements from 55 BC to the early eleventh century	
● Roman	2, 3, 4, 5, 6, 19, 20
● Anglo-Saxon	2, 16,17, 19, 20
● Viking	2, 18, 19, 20
One invasion in greater depth – Roman	
● Land, trade	3, 14
● Everyday life	7, 8, 9, 10, 12, 13, 14, 15
● Houses and home life	7, 13, 15, 19
● Religious life	11, 16
● Place names/language	9, 10, 13, 14, 20
● Myths and legends	6, 11
● Art and architecture	7, 9, 11, 13, 15, 19

USING THE BOOK

The following paragraphs give a brief explanation of how the activity sheets and the different sections

in the teacher's notes work.

Activity sheets

In general, the activities are suitable for individual, group or class work. The activity sheets are intended to provide stimuli to both teachers and pupils which may then lead to the development of individual or group historical enquiry. The sheets are not intended to be worked through methodically: teachers will wish to select and adapt the activities and ideas to suit the needs of the children.

The resource sheets at the back of the book are intended to supplement particular activity sheets; indication is given in the teacher's notes if and when a resource sheet may be relevant.

Teacher's notes

● The *Skills* section lists the historical skills which the children will be developing in working on the activity sheet.

● The *National Curriculum* charts only indicate the Attainment Targets which will be studied through working on the activity sheet. Attainment targets covered by extension activities. and cross-curricular work are not listed in these charts.

● The *Background information* section gives useful historical information, particularly highlighting some areas with which children may be unfamiliar.

● The *Introductory work* section gives suggestions for pre-experience and ways of introducing the sheet.

● The *Using the sheet* section details any equipment children might need, explains what the children are expected to do and suggestions for prompting questions or activites to help them get the most out of the activity sheet.

● The *Extension activities* often include suggestions for cross-curricular activities and ways of developing the skills and knowledge promoted by the activity sheet.

Investigating History should not be seen as the entire scheme of work for a project. Children should also have the opportunity to handle and examine artefacts and original documentation and, if possible, to visit sites and museums which will further enrich their studies. They should also have access to research and information books which will allow them to investigate particular areas of interest.

RESOURCES

Pupil information books

General
Archaeology, C Goff, Macdonald
The Invaders, R Burrell, Oxford University Press

General introduction

The Romans

'Aspects of Roman Life' is a series by Longman which includes titles like *The Roman Army, Roman Towns* etc.

Ancient Rome, S James, Dorling Kindersley

Catus – A Child in Roman Britain AD80, T Woodbridge, Oxford

City – A Story of Roman Planning and Construction, D Macaulay, Collins

Everyday Life in Roman Britain, M and C H B Quenell, Batsford

Face to Face: Romans and Celts, F Macdonald, Simon & Schuster Young Books

Growing up in Roman Britain, P Wilkins, Batsford

Illustrated History of The World: Vol 2, Simon & Schuster Young Books

Inside Story: A Roman Villa, Simon & Schuster Young Books

Life in Roman Britain, A Birley, Batsford

Roman Cities, R Coote, Wayland

Roman Roads, P Warner, Wayland

Roman Soldiers, R Matthews, Wayland

The Roman Army, Peter Connolly, Simon & Schuster Young Books

The Romans – Activity Book, British Museum Publications

The Time Traveller's Book of Rome and the Romans, Usborne

What Do We Know About the Romans?, M Corbishley, Simon & Schuster Young Books

The Vikings

Face to Face: Vikings and Saxons, F Macdonald, Simon & Schuster Young Books

Illustrated History of the World: Vol 3, Simon & Schuster Young Books

The Time Traveller's Book of the Viking Raiders, Usborne

The Vikings, Macdonald

The Vikings: Activity Book, British Museum Publications

Viking Britain, T Triggs, Wayland

Viking Explorers, R Matthews, Wayland

Viking Longboats, M Mulvihill, Gloucester Press

Viking Warriors, Wayland

What Do We Know About the Vikings?, J Defrates, Simon & Schuster Young Books

The Saxons

Illustrated History of the World: Vol 3, Simon & Schuster Young Books

Saxon Village, R Place, Wayland

The Anglo-Saxons: Activity Book, British Museum Publications

Roman Britain, M O'Connell, Wayland

Historical Fiction

The Eagle of the Ninth, The Silver Branch, The Lantern Bearers all by Rosemary Sutcliffe

The Bronze Sword, The Queen's Brooch, The Viking Saga all by Henry Treece

The Fires of the Kings, The Last Harper by Julian Atterton

Olaf the Viking, Elizabeth Laird

Teacher's information

Teacher's reference books

'Evidence in History' series (*The Romans, The Saxons, The Vikings*), Simon & Schuster Education

A Teacher's Guide to Learning from Objects, Durbin, Morris and Wilkinson, English Heritage

Ancient Rome, S James, Dorling Kindersley

Archaeological Detectives: Poster Games, English Heritage

Archaeological Resources Handbook for Teachers, M J Corbishley, Council for British Archaeology

Archaeology for Schools booklets, Council for British Archaeology

In Search of History – Early Times, 1066, J Arnold

Saxon Britain, T Trigg, Wayland

The Roman World, M Corbishley, Kingfisher Books

Posters/Maps

Ordnance Survey Map of Roman Britain

Ordnance Survey Map of Hadrian's Wall

A Viking Settlement, History timeline: Romans to Victorians, Families in History: Romans to Victorians, all from Pictorial Charts

Computer software

The Saxons – Simulation program following the lives of an imaginary Saxon family (Garland), BBC, Archimedes, RM Nimbus

Viking England – A set of four programs: 'The Raiders', 'Journey's End', 'The Move' and 'The Jarl', simulating Viking England from raid to settlement (Fernleaf Educational Software), BBC, RM Nimbus

Useful addresses/Places to visit

British Museum, Great Russell Street, London WC1

Chedworth Roman Villa, Yanworth, Cheltenham (0242 89256)

English Heritage, Education Service, Keysign House, 429 Oxford Street, London W1R 2HD

Fishbourne Roman Palace, Chichester (0243 785859)

Housesteads Roman Fort, Hadrian's Wall, Northumberland

Jorvik Viking Centre, York

Museums Association, 34 Bloomsbury Way, London WC1A 2SA

Roman Baths, Bath

Verulanium Museum, St Albans (0727 59919)

Weald and Downland Open-Air Museum, Singleton (reconstructed Saxon village)

Historical introduction

To the Romans, Britain was a mysterious and unknown island, lying off the rim of the known world yet not completely beyond the bounds of civilisation. In fact, many of Britain's inhabitants were descended from the peoples of what is now northern France and Belgium, sharing the same culture. They were not blue-painted savages but, in the south at least, well-organised and quite technically accomplished societies. Divided into tribal kingdoms, they spoke a Celtic language, lived in large permanent settlements, and cultivated the soil with skill.

Their first contact with the expanding Roman Empire was in 55 BC when Julius Caesar, after conquering Gaul, led an expedition to Britain. He landed near Dover but penetrated only a few miles inland. The following year he returned with a larger force, defeated the main British tribe in the south, the Catuvellauni, and returned to Gaul after making a treaty with the Britons in which they acknowledged Roman influence and agreed to pay an annual tribute.

Over the next eighty years this relationship was maintained. Trade between the Roman Empire and Britain grew. The aristocracy of the prosperous southern tribes acquired a taste for Roman luxury goods; large jars of wine from Spain and Italy, and jewellery, ivory and glassware crossed into Britain. In return there was a steady flow of cattle, corn, slaves, gold, iron, hides, pearls and clever hunting dogs from Britain to the Roman Empire. This satisfactory state of affairs lasted until AD 43 when the Emperor Claudius decided to invade – and this time to conquer.

A Roman army of 40,000 men landed at Richborough in Kent. They marched inland, defeated an army of combined British tribes and then crossed the Thames to capture the capital of the Catuvellauni at Colchester.

They conquered the rest of Britain remarkably quickly. By AD 47 most of the lowlands had been occupied. This was partly because the different tribes found it impossible to combine against the invaders, and some tribes submitted without even a fight. Roman success was also due to the vast superiority of their military force. The Britons were individually brave, their chariots spectacular and their weapons beautifully crafted but all this was no match for the disciplined efficiency of the only professional army in the ancient world. But above all, the superior supply arrangements of the Romans enabled them to maintain their troops in the field at all times when the tribal warriors had to return to their farms after a short time.

The only serious resistance to the Romans came from Caratacus, the king of the Catuvellauni, who fled to the west and roused the tribes there. But the remorseless pressure of the Roman advance drove him from one stronghold to another until he was defeated, betrayed and captured.

While the legions pushed back the frontiers, the occupied areas were organised into a Roman province. London was founded as a trading post and supply depot, a colony of retired soldiers was established at Colchester and small settlements began to grow around the legionary fortresses. The Romans began to exploit the resources of their new colony, and trade increased. Some of the Britons began to adopt Roman attitudes as well as using their goods, but the vast majority of the population lived untouched by Roman civilisation.

This smooth and apparently inevitable process was violently disrupted in AD 60 by the rebellion of the Iceni from East Anglia led by their queen, Boudicca, when the Romans came very close to losing their new province. The Iceni had been apparently content with Roman rule and it was only the greed and criminal insensitivity of the Roman administrators that prompted their rebellion. When Boudicca's husband, King Prasutagus, died he willed half his considerable fortune to the Emperor Nero in the hope that his widow and daughters would be allowed to enjoy the rest. But Roman officials behaved with insufferable brutality, flogging the queen and raping her daughters. The Iceni determined to avenge this insult, armed themselves and swept down towards Colchester, where they were joined by the Trinovantes who had been enduring the arrogant behaviour of the retired soldiers in the colony at Colchester. The veterans were all killed and the town destroyed. The triumphant horde then marched on to lay waste to London and Verulamium (St Albans) before being crushingly defeated. Boudicca took poison and died.

This was the most extensive and dangerous setback to Roman rule. Over the next century the remaining hostile tribes were subdued and the Romanisation of much of the lowlands consolidated. In AD 122 Hadrian's Wall was completed and the northern frontier fixed for the remainder of the Roman occupation.

A network of roads, well-engineered and mainly straight, crossed the country. Originally built to move the legions about, they also stimulated trade. Towns flourished and by the second century there was a small but fully developed urban society for the first time in Britain. Roman towns were small, with the exception of London, but they all contained what we expect to find in any place that defines itself as a town. They had shops and industries, places of worship and entertainment, law courts, centres of administration and the organisation to maintain their facilities and govern their citizens.

Most of their inhabitants were Britons, Romanised to varying degrees. Latin was written and spoken by an educated minority and some British nobles went so far in their identification with Rome as to abandon their trousers for the toga. Being part of an empire that stretched to the deserts of Arabia brought to Britain a wide variety of peoples. There were

Historical introduction

patrician Roman administrators, Greek doctors, Spanish merchants, Syrian archers and slaves from all over the known world, but these were only an exotic crust on the overwhelming Celtic mass of the rural population.

Roman civilisation extended to the countryside where wealthy Romans and Britons built villas. Some of these were the equivalent of the 18th century country house, a gentleman's residence of great opulence, but others were working estates. The larger ones were often quite luxurious with mosaic floors, frescoes on the walls and, of course, underfloor heating.

The prosperity of Roman Britain was at its peak in the middle of the 4th century when the rest of the Empire was in serious decline. Rome was threatened by incursions of Barbarians and almost continual civil war.

Britain began to be attacked by Saxon pirates from across the North Sea in the second half of the 4th century. The countermeasures included building a line of forts along the east and south coasts and organising sea patrols with ingeniously camouflaged ships. These measures held until 367 when the Barbarians for the first time co-ordinated their actions and made a joint attack on Britain. Scots and Picts poured over Hadrian's Wall while Saxons descended on the coast. For over a year, bands of brigands roamed the length of Britain until a task force arrived from Gaul to restore order. The town defences were repaired and trade and industry restored to prosperity.

The collapse of Roman rule came at the end of the 4th century when the number of troops in Britain was progressively reduced. This was not, as is popularly thought, to provide troops for a last defence of Rome itself, but was the futile and selfish action of the military commanders to back their Imperial ambitions. The last troops left Britain for no nobler reason than to put a pretender on the Imperial throne.

With the end of any effective central government, however, a concerted defence against the Saxons became almost impossible. Town life and villa society in the country continued, but with diminished vigour as trade and industry slowly stuttered to a halt somewhere in the middle of the 5th century and Britain entered the period known, because of the paucity of any evidence, as 'The Dark Ages'.

Local potentates filled the vacuum left by Roman authority. Some were local landowners, others military men who had been invited to take control, or seized it, in order to resist the increasing attacks of the Saxons.

By 430 Saxons were arriving in increasing numbers and they were coming not to loot but to settle. They came from three closely related Germanic tribes living in what is now Denmark and northern Germany, being forced to migrate by the poverty of their own land. The Jutes, the smallest of the three tribes, settled in Kent and parts of Hampshire. The Saxons, the largest tribe, occupied the west and south of England, while the Angles settled in East Anglia, the Midlands and the north. They came to join the first Saxon settlers, who were not invaders at all but mercenary soldiers hired by the Romans. The British successors to the Romans kept up the practice of hiring mercenaries, and Vortigern, the ruler of southern England, is reputed to have invited the Jutish princes Hengist and Horsa who eventually overthrew him and founded the Kingdom of Kent.

For the rest of the century there was continual warfare between the Britons and invading Saxons. A major British victory in c. 500 at Mons Badonicus, an unknown location but probably somewhere in the south-west, stemmed the tide for nearly a generation but then the Saxons continued to advance. During this time the fragile infrastructure of Roman civilisation finally withered away. It is significant that archaeological evidence shows that far more villas simply rotted and collapsed than were violently destroyed.

By 600 seven Saxon and three British kingdoms had emerged. The Britons had been pushed back to the western fringes and their kingdoms occupied Wales, Cornwall and the north-west. The rest of the country was in Saxon hands.

The Saxons were farmers and had little use for the towns, which in the main simply decayed, although because they tended to occupy strategic sites at river crossings or crossroads and they had the remains of strong defences, they were never completely abandoned. Only in very rare cases, like Caistor St Edmunds near Norwich, was occupation never resumed. The seven Saxon kingdoms fought among themselves until by 800 the Kingdom of Mercia ruled by Offa was dominant. Trade increased and the growing Church fostered something of an educational revival.

It is ironic that the Saxons, growing comfortable and taking the first crude steps to emulate the Roman civilisation they had helped destroy, should be attacked in their turn by pagan tribes forced to leave barren homelands. In 789 the first Vikings landed on the south coast and by the next century brutal plundering raids were a terrifying annual occurence.

The Vikings who ravaged England were mainly Danish. At first they came to loot but from the 850s onwards simple robbery gave way to conquest and settlement. In 865 the Danish 'Great Army', led by Ivarr the Boneless, landed in East Anglia. Within four years this army had killed the kings of Northumbria and East Anglia, conquered their lands and was ready to march on Wessex. This moment of supreme crisis produced a leader worthy of it in Alfred the Great. At first he could only save Wessex by buying the Danes off, which gave him a five-year respite while the Danes conquered Mercia. This left

Historical introduction

Wessex the last truly independent Saxon kingdom. Eventually the Danes returned to attack Wessex and were defeated. Their leader Guthrum made peace with Alfred who recognised that the Danes occupied much of northern and eastern England and agreed that this should be independent and known as the Danelaw. Once settled, mainly in Yorkshire and Lincolnshire, the Danes proved to be excellent farmers and diligent traders.

Alfred spent the rest of his reign building up a system of defence against the Danes, based on fortified frontier strongholds known as *burhs*, as well as instituting a very necessary revival of learning and literacy to repair the damage wrought by the wholesale destruction of monasteries.

When Alfred died in 899 England was divided into three separate kingdoms: Wessex included all of southern and western England, with its northern boundary at Bedford; English Mercia, ruled by Alfred's son-in-law, covered the West Midlands and most of Wales; all of eastern England from the Thames to the Tees was under Danish rule. There were also Norwegian settlements on the north-west coast and in south Wales.

Over the next half century Alfred's successors gradually reduced the extent of the Viking territory and built up their own power throughout England, so the country was effectively united when Edgar died in 975. He was eventually succeeded by his son Ethelred 'the Unready', whom history has treated very harshly. He obviously lacked many of the qualities necessary for successful kingship but England would probably have prospered had it not been for the return of the Vikings.

England's wealth lured the raiders from Scandinavia in growing numbers, fiercer and better disciplined than ever before. They inflicted several heavy defeats on the Saxons and could only be induced to go away by huge bribes. This of course just brought them back for more. After Ethelred had ordered the massacre of the inhabitants of the Danelaw, it was hardly surprising that the survivors welcomed Swein, King of Norway, when he landed bent on conquest in 1013.

Swein's invasion left only the original Wessex in Saxon hands. Ethelred fled and soon died, and when his son Edmund died, Swein's son Cnut (Canute of the waves story) became King of England, Denmark and Norway. Cnut was not in England much but he continued the civilising mission of the Saxon kings with great enthusiasm and energy, founding monasteries, fostering scholarship and making laws. When Cnut died, shortly followed by both his sons, almost everyone wanted to restore the dynasty of Wessex, and Ethelred's son Edward (the nickname 'the Confessor' was given him because of his extreme religiosity) was elected king in 1042.

Edward ruled indifferently until 1066 and died without an heir. This precipitated a great crisis. The King of Norway, Harold Hardrada, and William, Duke of Normandy, both announced their intention to invade and take the throne. The English elected Harold Godwin, Edward's brother-in-law, king. Although not of royal blood he was experienced in warfare and the best man for such dangerous times. When the Vikings landed, Harold defeated them near York, but then he had to hurry south to meet the Duke of Normandy. On 14 October 1066, near Hastings, he was killed and the Saxons defeated. The Normans, the last successful invaders of England, had triumphed and the Saxon dominion, that stretched back to Hengist and Horsa and had survived successive Viking assaults, disappeared for good.

Activity Sheets
and
Teacher's Notes

1 Archaeology

Skills

Using historical evidence
Reconstructing the past from evidence

Attainment targets

Level	AT 1	AT 2	AT 3
2			↓
3			
4			
5			

Introductory work

To introduce the children to the sheet you could show them a broken plate and ask them to guess what they think it is before having a go at piecing it together. They could then make up a story about where they think it was found and why they think it was buried there. This can then lead on to a discussion about the role of the archaeologist whose job it is to 'dig' things up, piece them together and deduce clues from what they find. Your local museum or archaeological society may have information about finds discovered in the local area or an archaeologist could be invited into the classroom to talk about his/her work. They might be able to bring some finds with them and show the children the tools they use.

See teacher's resources section at the front of this book for further information.

Using the sheet

On this first sheet we meet Professor Pick and Dr. Shovel who will appear throughout the pupil activity sheets and introduce children to the idea of *evidence*.

The object on the sheet is a Roman tombstone and might have been found outside the gates of a Roman town.

Children will need scissors, glue and card. If they stick the pieces onto card it will be easier to piece them together. The size of the object can be worked out using the scale at the bottom of the sheet, possibly comparing this with a similar modern object to get an idea of the size.

Discussion could then be guided by the teacher on questions such as: What do you think the object was used for? Can you think of a modern object like this one? How is the object decorated? What clues does the decoration give?

Extension activities

1   Children could reconstruct the tombstone using clay. They could try to make it to the correct size and include the decoration.
2   Children could use information books to research other 'Roman' objects and make their own jigsaws for a friend to try to reconstruct.
3   You could encourage discussion about where the tombstone might have been found and this could lead into a story-writing exercise about how the object ended up there and why it was in pieces.
4   Children could design and make a monument to themselves, showing how they would like to be depicted and what achievements they would want recorded.
5   School archaeology. The class could be divided into two groups. Each goes off to opposite ends of the playing field and buries some broken objects. Later, they go and dig up each other's finds and write a report about their discoveries. Each group then tells the other whether their deductions were correct. This activity will give the children lots of opportunity for measuring, recording and deducing work.

Archaeology

Archaeologists like Professor Pick and Dr. Shovel are hardly ever lucky enough to find something in one piece.
Here are the bits of an important find. Cut them out neatly and try to fit them together. What is it?
Work out the actual size of the object using this scale.

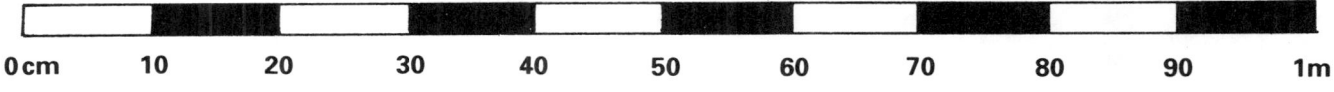

2 Invasions

Teacher's notes

Skills

Using historical evidence
Chronological ordering
Reconstructing the past from evidence

Attainment targets

Level	AT 1	AT 2	AT 3
2			
3	↓		
4			
5			

Introductory work

It would be helpful if the children could do some work on chronology before starting this sheet. They could make a timeline of their own life putting on significant events, e.g. started school, sister born. Another way of helping them understand 'a long time ago' is to unravel a toilet roll or two, telling them each sheet represents, say, ten years. When the roll has reached the playground they will begin to see just how long ago these invasions took place.

You might like to introduce the sheet by reading an extract from Henry Treece's *Legions of the Eagle*, which tells the story of a boy living in Britain at the time of the first Roman invasion, or Rosemary Sutcliffe's *The Lantern Bearers*, which is about the Saxon invasion of Britain.

Using the sheet

Children could start by putting the dates of the invasions on a timeline. They may need to have the term AD (Anno Domini, in the year of our Lord) explained to them. They could discuss how the ships and boats of the four groups of invaders differ.

The illustrations on the map show what resources the invaders came to Britain to take advantage of. Another reason for invasion was the desire for fame and glory. This was mostly a Roman motivation and is something which could be brought out in discussion.

Extension activities

1 Children could do some background reading to find other reasons why people invaded and how long the invasions lasted. Each invasion only lasted a few hundred years. Why? Reasons include: new threats from the continent, problems with revolting tribes in Britain, and, for the Romans, problems of controlling a huge empire.
2 Children could write about how it feels to be one of the members of an invading group, or how it feels to be a Briton living on the coast and witnessing the arrival of an invading group.
3 There are many other activities which can be used to reinforce an understanding of chronology: ordering time measurements from smallest to largest (e.g. minute, hour, day, year, decade, . . .); putting dates in order (e.g. significant dates from this century); putting pieces of evidence with dates on (e.g. coins, newspapers) into chronological order; putting personal and family photographs and belongings into chronological order.

Invasions

Britain has been invaded a number of times. Why do you think people wanted to invade Britain? Make a list of the reasons you can see in this picture.

Vikings 860-1000

Saxons 400-600

COAL

good farmland

for sale

gold

lead

silver

iron

tin

oysters

Normans 1066

Romans AD 43

3 The Roman invasion

Skills

Chronological ordering
Making a timechart
Identifying different types of cause and consequence

Attainment targets

Level	AT 1	AT 2	AT 3
2			
3			
4			
5			

Background information

Before the invasion of AD 43, Julius Ceasar had made an expedition to Britain in 55 BC. His army defeated the Britons but didn't advance far into Britain. The following year he was back, marched inland and forced the British tribes to make peace. However, there were problems across the Channel in Gaul and Caesar was forced to withdraw, never to return.

Britain was left alone for over 90 years until AD 43 when Emperor Claudius saw the conquest of Britain as a good chance to win a great victory. Claudius only stayed a couple of weeks but the army remained fighting and eventually conquered Britain.

Using the sheet

This sheet should be worked on after *Invasions* (2) to build on the skills of chronological ordering and to follow up one of the invasions in more depth. The timeline the children have to produce is on a large scale which could be compared to a personal timeline.

You should emphasise that in the pictures only Caratacus' tribe is shown fighting when there were in fact many British tribes who fought the Romans. This was why they found it so hard to defeat the organised Roman army.

Children will need scissors and possibly a long strip of coloured paper on which they can arrange the pictures in chronological order. They could then draw the timeline onto the coloured paper. The children can either order the dates or the actions in the pictures.

As an alternative to drawing a timeline the children could make a timeclock where the dates of the invasion are placed within a circle like a clock rather than on a line.

The cut-out pictures could be used on the timeline/timeclock or the children could redraw them on a smaller scale.

Extension activities

1 It might be useful to put up a big timeline on the classroom wall showing the events of the Roman invasion. As the topic advances other dates/events could be added.

2 The story of the Roman invasion can be retold in various ways, e.g. as a piece of narrative writing, in diary form (from the point of view of a soldier in the Roman/British army), in children's own strip cartoons or newspaper reports.

3 Using a map of Europe, plot the route the Roman ships may have taken to get to Britian and where they landed. Other mapwork might include plotting on a map of Europe/Northern Africa the other countries that were invaded by the Romans and which became part of the Roman Empire. The Roman and modern names of countries could be contrasted. Links here with *Roads and trade* (14) which looks at trade within the Empire.

 # The Roman invasion

In AD 43 the Roman army invaded Britain.
Draw your own timeline for the Roman invasion. Cut out the
pictures below and fit them on your timeline in the right order.

AD 43–46

The Britons are defeated.

AD 51

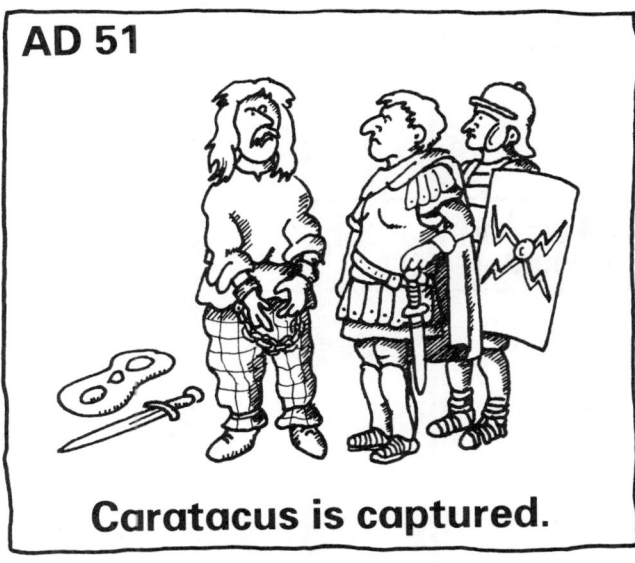

Caratacus is captured.

May AD 43

The Romans land in Kent.

AD 55–100

The Romans build towns.

May AD 43

The Roman army sets sail.

AD 46–51

**A few Britons go on fighting
led by Caratacus.**

4 The Roman army

Skills

Using historical evidence
Making deductions from evidence

Attainment targets

Level	AT 1	AT 2	AT 3
2			↓
3			
4			
5			

Background information

It might be useful to do some preliminary work on the Roman army, introducing words such as centurion, cohort, legion, etc. The diagram below may help clarify the set-up and could be reproduced larger for the classroom wall.

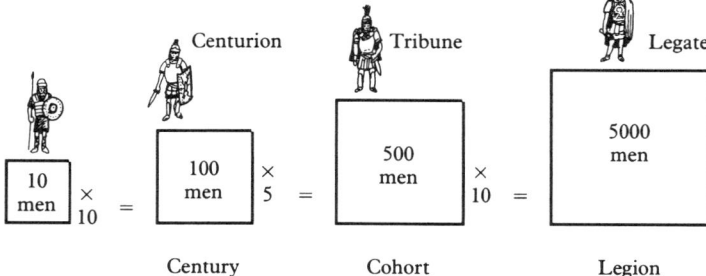

Using the sheet

The children will need scissors, coloured crayons and a thin strip of card to help reinforce the soldier so he will stand up. The whole cut-out could be stuck onto card to make it stronger. It is important that children use appropriate colours to colour the soldier so they should take note of the materials from which his uniform was made. Children could discuss why different materials were used for different parts of the uniform.

The picture showing the Romans fighting will pick up on the organised nature of the Roman army and can be contrasted with the next sheet on *The British warriors* (5) who look disorganised by comparison.

Extension activities

1 There are many areas of research that could be undertaken, e.g. weapons, different methods of fighting, the Roman army on the march, Roman roads, setting up camp, the development of forts (you might be lucky and have a local Roman fort/town nearby, or the children could make a model of a Roman fort).
2 Technology work could involve making a Roman war machine like a catapult which would fire a stone (lump of Plasticine) a certain distance.
3 Hadrian's Wall was built by the Roman army to keep the Scottish Picts out of Roman Britain. The children could draw a long picture/model of the wall to go right round the classroom. It could also replicate the actual building as groups of children could be responsible for different sections just as the legionaries were. The wall could even have soldiers on it – you can buy little plastic models of Roman soldiers quite cheaply.

The Roman army

A Roman soldier was called a legionary because the Roman army was divided into legions. There were about 5000 men in each legion.

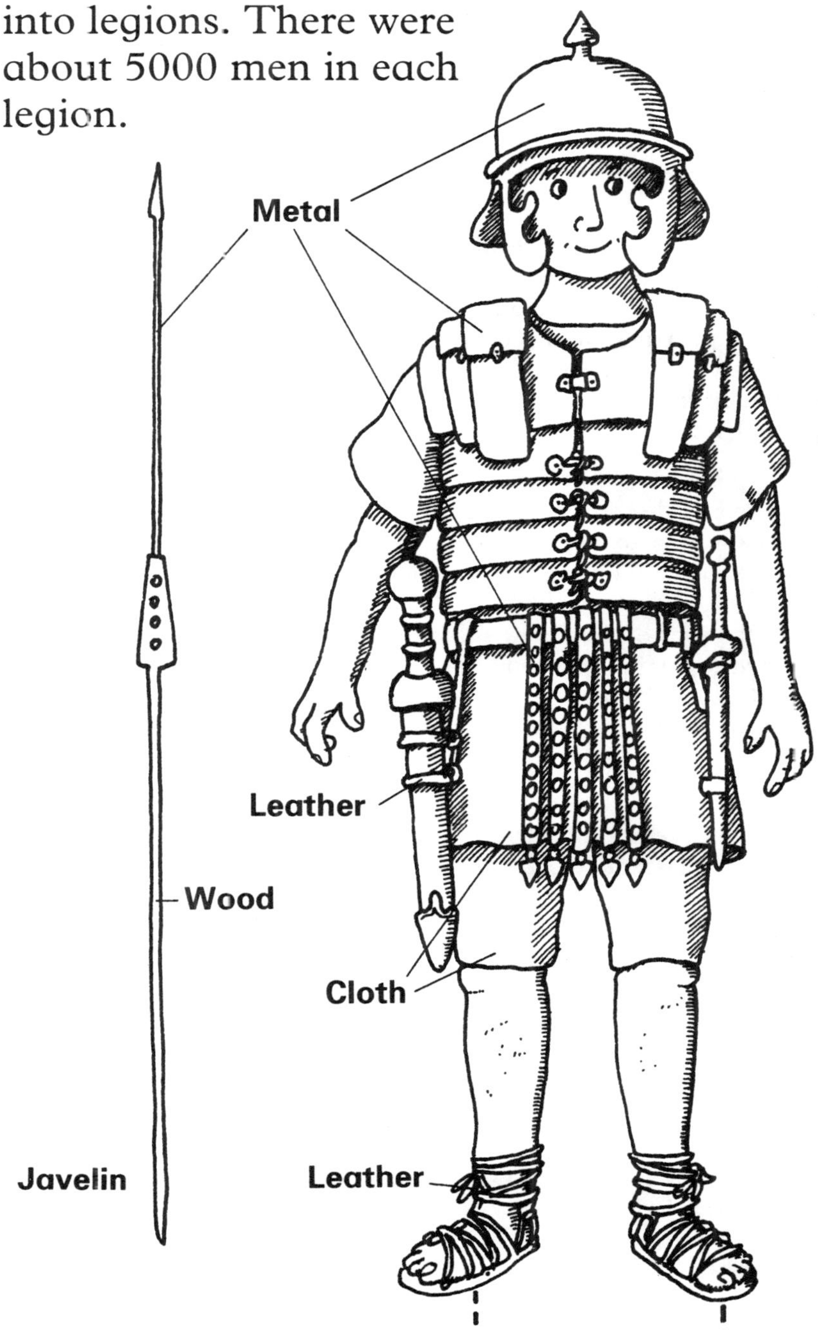

Metal

Leather

Wood

Cloth

Javelin

Leather

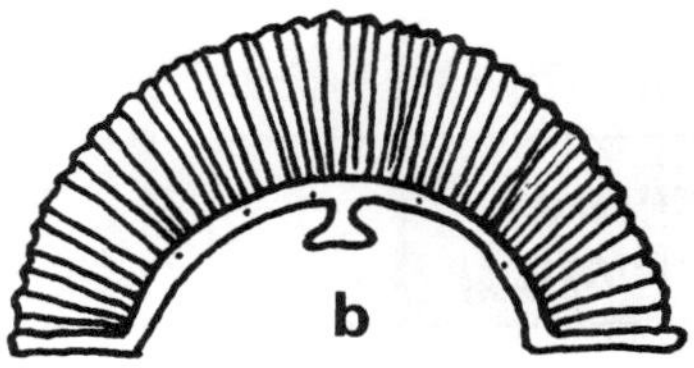

b

a

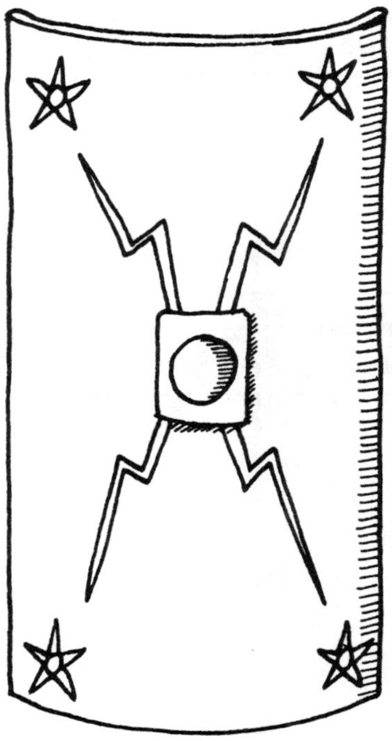

Shield

Tab

Colour the soldier, thinking about what his uniform is made of. Cut him out making sure you include the tab so he will stand up.

You can make this soldier a Centurion by putting the staff (a) in his hand and the crest (b) on his helmet. Find out the link between the words century and centurion.

5 The British warriors

Skills

Using historical evidence
Making deductions from evidence
Identifying similarities and differences

Attainment targets

Level	AT 1	AT 2	AT 3
2			
3	↓		↓
4			
5			

Background information

When the Romans arrived in Britain they found a country composed of many different tribes. The main tribes which the Romans initially encountered were the Catuvellauni (South of England), the Iceni (East Anglia) and the Trinovantes (London area and Essex). The tribes, although brave and fiercely defensive of their territory, found it impossible to combine against the organised Romans and many settlements gave up without a fight.

Using the sheet

Children will need scissors, coloured pencils and a thin strip of card to stick to the warrior to make him stand up. It is important that the children take note of the materials his outfit is made of before colouring him in.

One of the aims of this sheet is to provide a comparison with *The Roman army* (4) and to give some clues as to why the Romans were able to conquer Britain. Children should pick up on things such as the warlike and primitive nature of the tribes and their disorganised way of fighting.

Extension activites

1 Many battles were fought between the Roman and British armies which could be researched. From this the children could write news reports or tape radio reports of the battles as if they were eye witnesses.
2 On a map of Britain, children could plot where the British tribes lived and the sites of the more important battles between the Romans and Britons.
3 Some tribes of British warriors are reputed to have painted their faces and bodies with blue dye (woad) to make themselves look more frightening. Do the children think this would have been effective? Children could make up their own face-painting designs to frighten the Romans away.
4 Children could make their own shield out of cardboard and decorate it with swirling Celtic patterns.

The British warriors

Colour in this picture of a British warrior. Cut him out making sure you include the tab so he will stand up.

The British warriors fought very bravely in battle but the Romans easily defeated them. Why do you think the Roman army won? Make a list of the differences between the Roman soldiers and the British warriors.

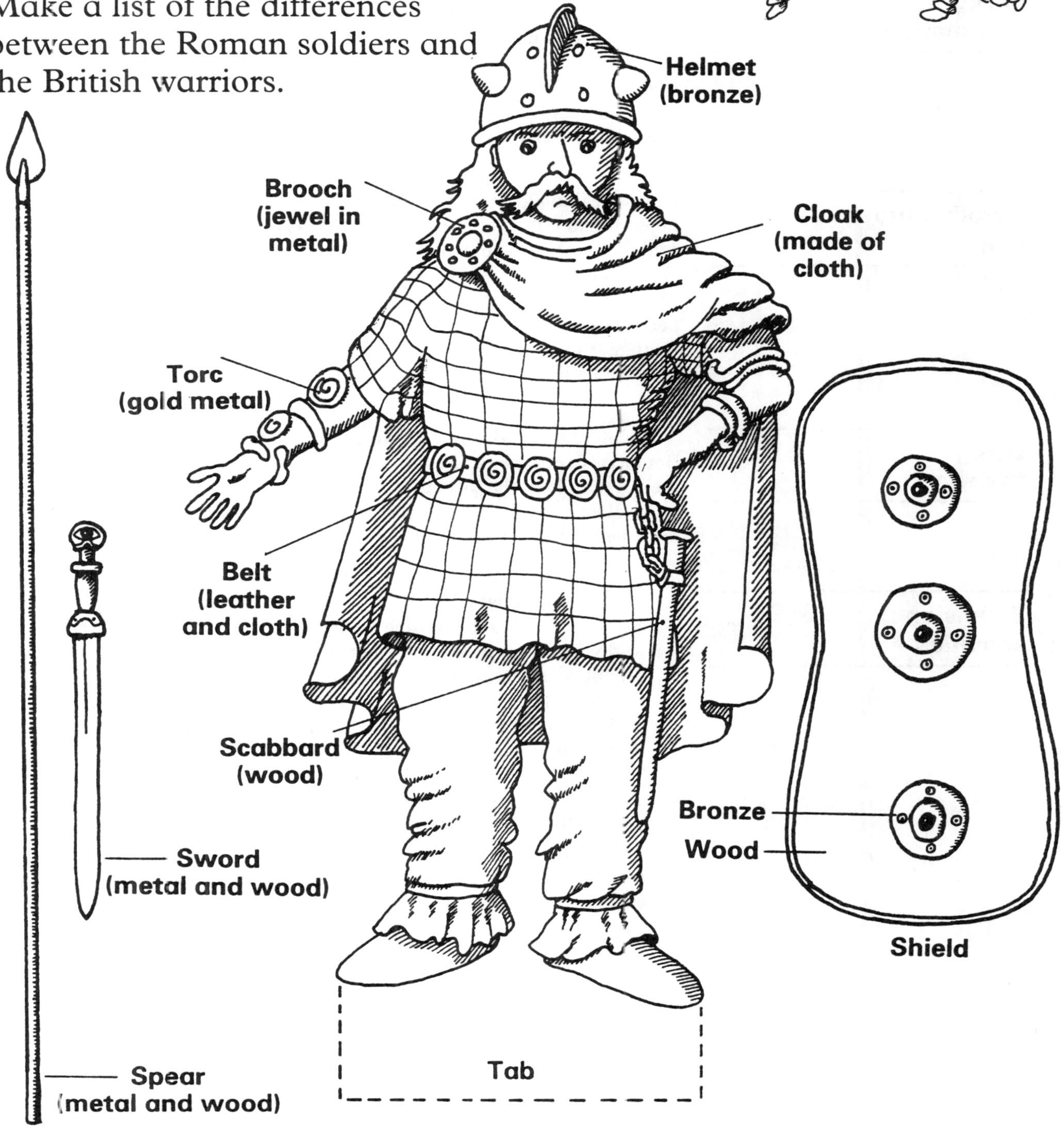

Helmet (bronze)

Brooch (jewel in metal)

Cloak (made of cloth)

Torc (gold metal)

Belt (leather and cloth)

Scabbard (wood)

Sword (metal and wood)

Bronze

Wood

Shield

Tab

Spear (metal and wood)

6 Boudicca's revolt

Skills

Using historical evidence
Reconstructing the past from evidence
Comparing two pieces of evidence

Attainment targets

Level	AT 1	AT 2	AT 3
2			↓
3		↓	
4			
5			

Background information

For a fuller account of the story of Boudicca, or Boadicea as she is sometimes known, see the historical outline in the *Introduction*. She has become very much a legendary figure, especially since the only evidence we have about her was written by Roman historians and their writings were very much based on hearsay.

The extract by Tacitus comes from his book *The Annals of Imperial Rome*. This was written in the early 2nd century AD.

Introductory work

Before beginning this sheet it might be useful to discuss with the children how we find out about people from the past. You could compare the little evidence we have about Boudicca with what we have about someone like Queen Victoria, for whom we have an abundance of literary, pictorial and photographic evidence. It might also be useful to point out the differences between *primary* and *secondary* evidence – primary evidence is made or written at the time the events happened, secondary evidence is written or produced after the event.

Using the sheet

The children should read the two accounts carefully for clues about Boudicca's appearance. Because we have no primary pictorial evidence we are not sure how she looked. Their pictures will be right as long as they have taken note of the written evidence. They could draw her as a portrait or in battle with chariot, warriors etc.

Extension activities

1   The children might be able to find other portraits of Boudicca and compare them to the written evidence. A lot of older pictures are wildly innaccurate and show her wearing horns on her head and driving a chariot with scythes on the hub-caps.

You could read the children an extract from Henry Treece's fiction book *The Queen's Brooch* (about Boudicca) and discuss what impression of the queen comes over from this.

2   The question of how much we can trust different sorts of evidence is an interesting area to pursue. Both of the accounts of Boudicca are written by Roman historians. How might a British historian have described her and the battles that were fought? A game of 'Chinese whispers' is a good way of getting across to children the idea of how easily spoken evidence can change. (This can be likened to the way Tacitus and Dio would have found out about Boudicca.)

 # Boudicca's revolt

In AD 60 a British tribe called the Iceni revolted against
Roman rule. They were led by their queen, Boudicca. They
did terrible damage to the Romans before they were beaten.
Here are two accounts of Queen Boudicca written by
Roman historians. Using all the information on this page
draw a picture of what you think she looked like.

"She was huge ... with a harsh voice. A great mass of bright red hair fell to her knees. She wore a great twisted torc and a tunic of many colours, over which was a thick mantle, fastened by a brooch."

Dio

"Boudicca drove round in a chariot, her daughters with her. As she reached each tribe she said the Britons were used to being led into battle by women."

Tacitus

Torc
(gold necklace)

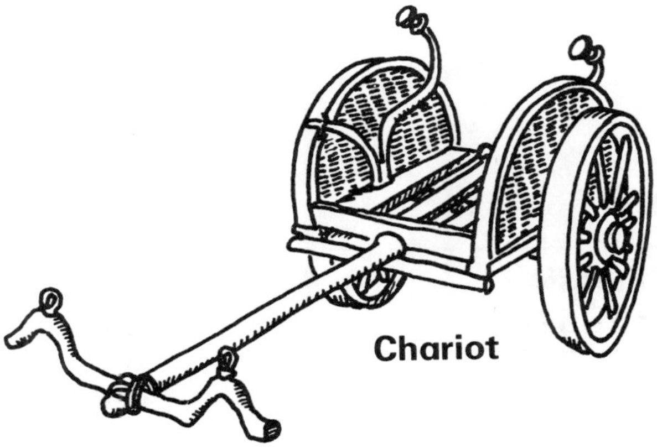

Chariot

Brooch

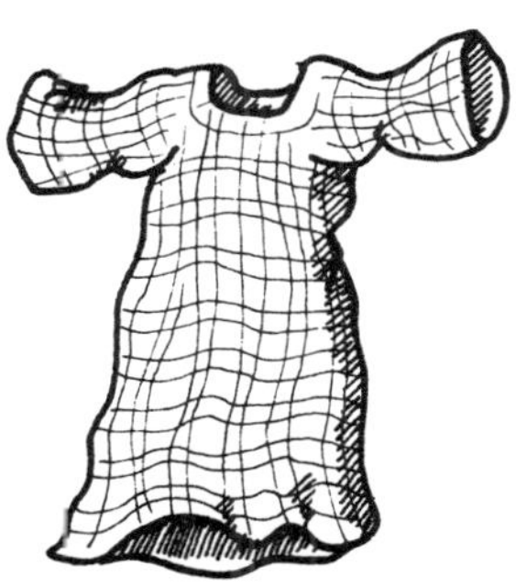

Tunic

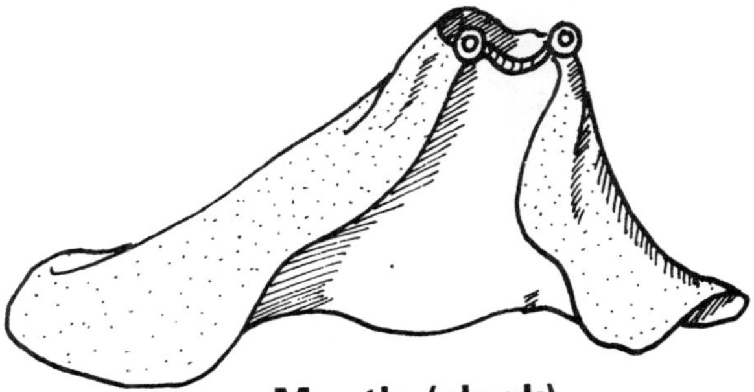

Mantle (cloak)

7 A Roman house

Skills

Using historical evidence
Making deductions from evidence
Identifying similarities and differences between past and present

Attainment targets

Level	AT 1	AT 2	AT 3
2			↓
3			
4	↓		
5			

Background information

Members of the Roman family on this sheet will appear on other sheets and useful work can be done on their names, their dress and the fact that they have a slave. Slavery is a difficult concept for young children to understand and may need considerable explanation.

Most slaves were captured in wars, although children who were abandoned or sold by their parents might also become slaves. Slaves were sold in the market place. Slaves with a trade cost more. Slaves were slaves for life but they could eventually buy their freedom or be freed by their masters. It was common to free slaves in a will. A slave's children automatically became slaves.

A slave's life depended greatly on their owner. A family slave like Hardalio might lead a fairly pleasant life, but a slave working in a mine in Roman Britain would have had a grim time.

Using the sheet

The main aim of this sheet is to compare a Roman house with a modern house, looking for similarities as well as differences. The children could either list the similarities and differences or tabulate the information taking a different aspect for each column, e.g. plan, front view, rooms, family.

The rooms in the Roman house may need some explanation. The shrine would be where the family kept its statues of household gods, the hypocaust is the Roman central heating system. The children may notice there is no bathroom. They could look at the sheet on *The baths* (9) for information about public baths.

Extension activities

1 Children could make models of Roman and modern houses.
2 Children could draw pictures of their own families standing outside their houses.
3 Many of the floors inside the Roman house would have been decorated with mosaic and the walls would have been painted. There are wonderful opportunities for design/art work here: children could imagine they are Roman decorators who have been called in by Julius Maximus to carry out research and then present their own design. Comparison with modern decoration and floor coverings could be made.

 # A Roman house

This picture shows a Roman family standing outside their Roman town house in Britain.

Julius Maximus   **Augusta**   **Valerius**   **Flavia**   **Hardalio (the slave)**

This is a plan of their house. Use the Latin dictionary to work out the names of the rooms.

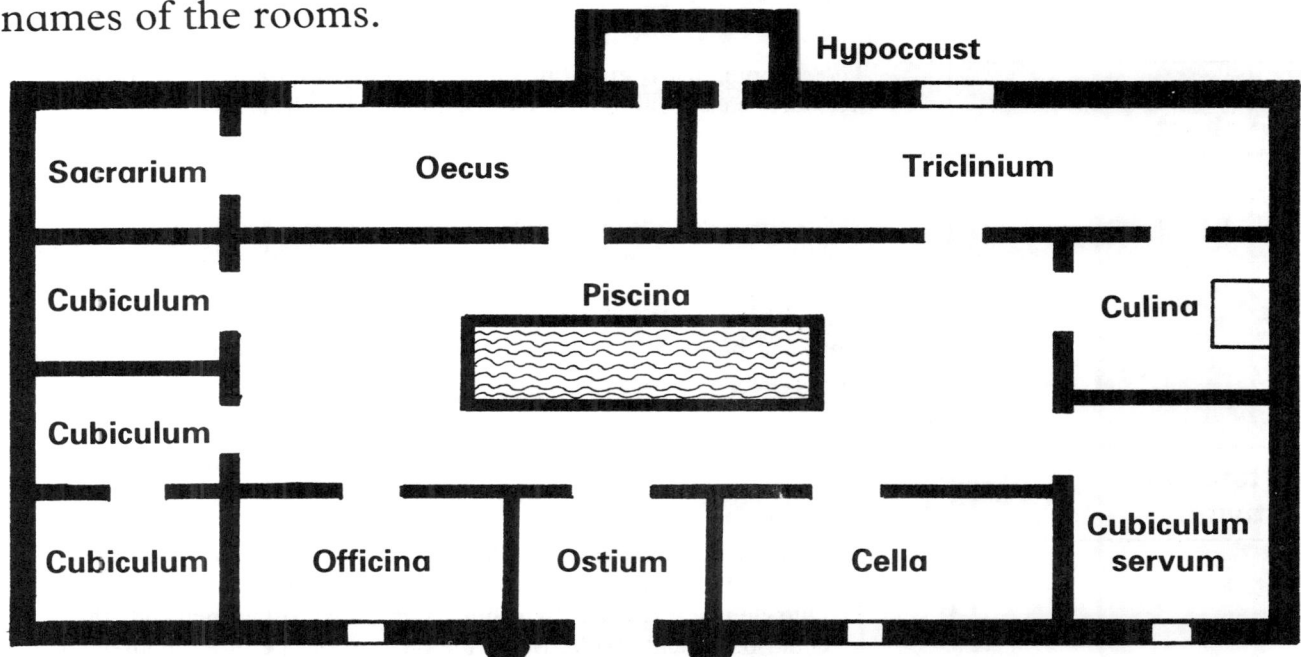

Hypocaust

Sacrarium	Oecus	Triclinium
Cubiculum	Piscina	Culina
Cubiculum		
Cubiculum	Officina Ostium	Cella Cubiculum servum

This is the plan and front view of a modern house in Britain.

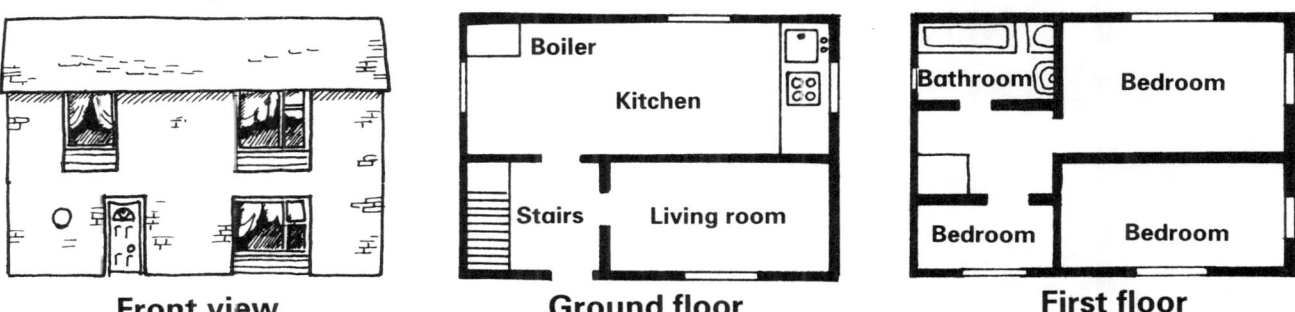

Front view   **Ground floor**   **First floor**

Boiler · Kitchen · Stairs · Living room · Bathroom · Bedroom · Bedroom · Bedroom

Make a list of things that are the same and things that are different between the Roman and the modern house.

8 Shopping

Skills

Using historical evidence
Identifying similarities and differences between past and present
Using historical language

Attainment targets

Level	AT 1	AT 2	AT 3
2			
3			
4	↓		↓
5			

Background information

There are no written accounts of what shopping in Romano-British towns was like. The evidence we have comes from archaeological remains, particularly carvings on stone and utensils, such as wine pots or corn mills.

Introductory work

As an introductory activity it might be useful to look at a plan of a Roman town, identifying where the shops are situated (see also *The Roman town* (13)). They were more like modern shopping arcades or markets than a high street of shops.

Using the sheet

The shopping list is in Latin. Children should use the Latin dictionary (Resource sheet 3) to translate the names of the items.

The children can either write on the sheet or redraw/cut out the pictures and label them. They will need to look closely for clues in the pictures to help them match the items on Hardalio's shopping list.

The sheet also asks for comparison with modern day shopping. This could be presented in tabular form or by drawing the modern shop beside the Roman one. It is important to encourage the children to identify the similarities as well as the differences. For example, we still have butchers' shops and bakeries – the methods of production may have changed but the basic principle is the same.

Extension activities

1 Children are often fascinated by the Latin names for things. They might want to give themselves Latin names!
2 Children could retell Hardalio's shopping trip in written form or as a strip cartoon, perhaps including how he feels about having to do the shopping and what happens to him on his shopping trip.
3 Outside many Roman shops hung signs, advertising the goods that could be bought inside. Using the pictures on the sheet children could design their own signs for Roman shops and compare them with modern shop signs and adverts.

 # Shopping

The list on the board reads:

I PANIS
II CALCEVS
III TEXTVM
IV VINVM
V CARNIS
VI HOLERIS

Hardalio, the family slave, has been sent out to do the shopping. Use the Latin dictionary to work out what is on his list. Write the name of the shop under each picture and decide where Hardalio would buy each of the items on his list. Where would Hardalio buy these things today?

9 The baths

Skills

Using historical evidence
Making deductions from evidence
Using historical language
Sequencing events

Attainment targets

Level	AT 1	AT 2	AT 3
2			↓
3			
4			
5			

Background information

Since most Roman houses did not have a bathroom, the public baths were an important feature of Roman towns. Men and women would go to the baths, either at different times or in separate facilities. Likening the baths to a modern leisure centre might help the children understand how Roman baths were probably used, i.e. for sport, socialising, saunas, massage, etc.

Seneca, a Roman writer, described the baths thus:

'On top of that, you've got the man who likes to hear his own voice in the bath or the chap who plunges into the swimming pool with an enormous splash, as well as the manicurist advertising his trade. The only time he stops his chatter is when he's plucking armpits – and then it's the customer who's screaming!'

Using the sheet

The Latin words for each room in the baths can be translated using the Latin dictionary (Resource sheet 3).

The pictures can either be matched on the sheet or cut out and rearranged in the correct order and then matched to the correct room. Although the task on the sheet asks the children to write a sentence by each picture, they could draw cartoon pictures, write an account in diary, story or drama/play form, or make a model or timeline from the plan.

Extension activities

1 Children could present a similar sequence for themselves visiting a modern day swimming pool. Similarities and differences between the old and the new baths could be discussed.

2 There are good potential links with Science here – children could investigate cold, warm and hot (frigidarium, tepidarium, calidarium).

3 Children could make a list of the people who work at the baths. They could use the picture clues on the sheet, the quote from Seneca and information books. Write beside the name of each job what they do, e.g. masseur – massages people, manicurist – plucks armpits and treats people's hands, furnace worker – keeps the fire going in the furnace.

The 'Time Traveller' book of *Rome and the Romans* (Usborne) gives a colourful double spread of an afternoon at the baths and a lot of pictorial information about the people who worked and visited there.

The baths

In Roman times the public baths were free to citizens of the town. People went there to meet friends as well as to get clean.

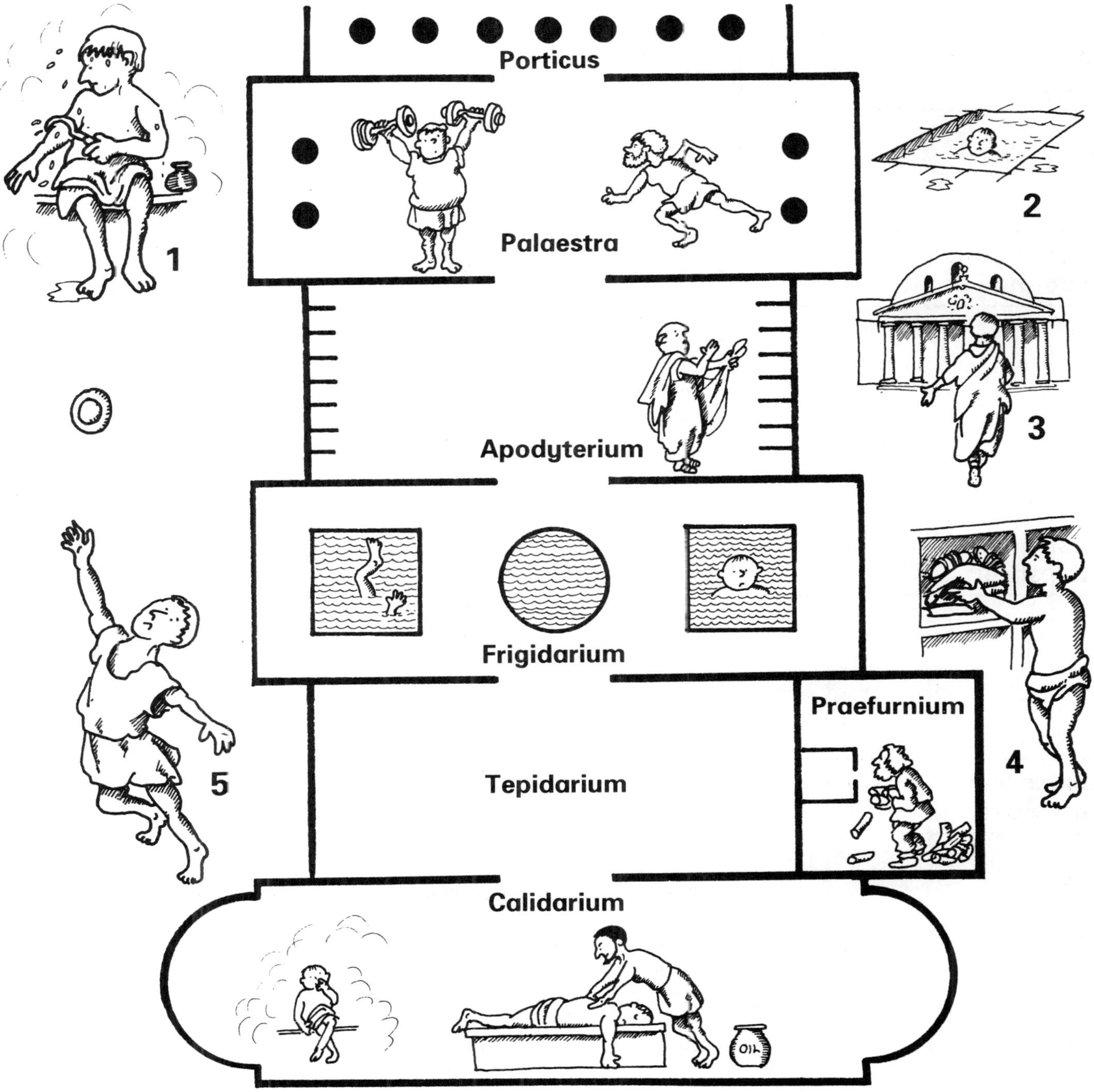

Porticus

Palaestra

1

2

Apodyterium

3

Frigidarium

Praefurnium

Tepidarium

5

4

Calidarium

The pictures of the things Julius did at the baths are muddled up. Try to put them in the right order. Match the numbered pictures to the rooms in the baths. Use the Latin dictionary to help you.

Write a sentence by each picture saying which room he is in and what he is doing.

10 Going to school

Skills

Using historical evidence
Identifying similarities and differences between past and present
Using historical language
Empathising with people of the past

Attainment targets

Level	AT 1	AT 2	AT 3
2			
3	↓		↓
4			
5			

Background information

Roman boys would start school at the age of six or seven. Very rich boys were tutored at home. The school day would begin very early every day of the week, with a break for lunch when the boys would go home. At primary level they would learn how to read, write and count; at secondary level they would study Latin, Greek, History, Geography, Astronomy, Geometry, Music and Public speaking.

It might be useful to do some work on Roman numerals before introducing this sheet. They are still used today (e.g. at the end of the credits on T.V. programmes, on buildings to commemorate the date of building, on statues and monuments, and in the front of some books).

Using the sheet

'Going to school' will be a topic with which the children will be able to empathise and they should identify similarities and differences between their own school life and Roman school life. Further discussion could include why they think only rich boys went to school and not girls or poor children.

The second task on the sheet asks the children to translate the Latin and work out the answer to Valerius' sums using the Latin dictionary (Resource sheet 3).

Extension activities

1   Children could make their own wax tablets using Plasticine or clay and scratch Latin messages to friends using a pencil or a stylus made out of a twig.
2   Children could discuss what they would have liked and disliked about going to a Roman school. Ask them to explain their answers.
3   Children could use information books to find out which games Roman children played (e.g. Jacks, hoops, or stick and ball games like hockey). Children could compare games played today with Roman games.
4   Drama/rôle-play work could involve reliving a day at a Roman school. You could hold your own Roman day, dressing in togas, doing Roman lessons, playing games, eating 'Roman' food, etc.

Only the sons of rich families went to school in Roman times.
Sometimes the teacher was a slave.
How is this classroom different from yours?

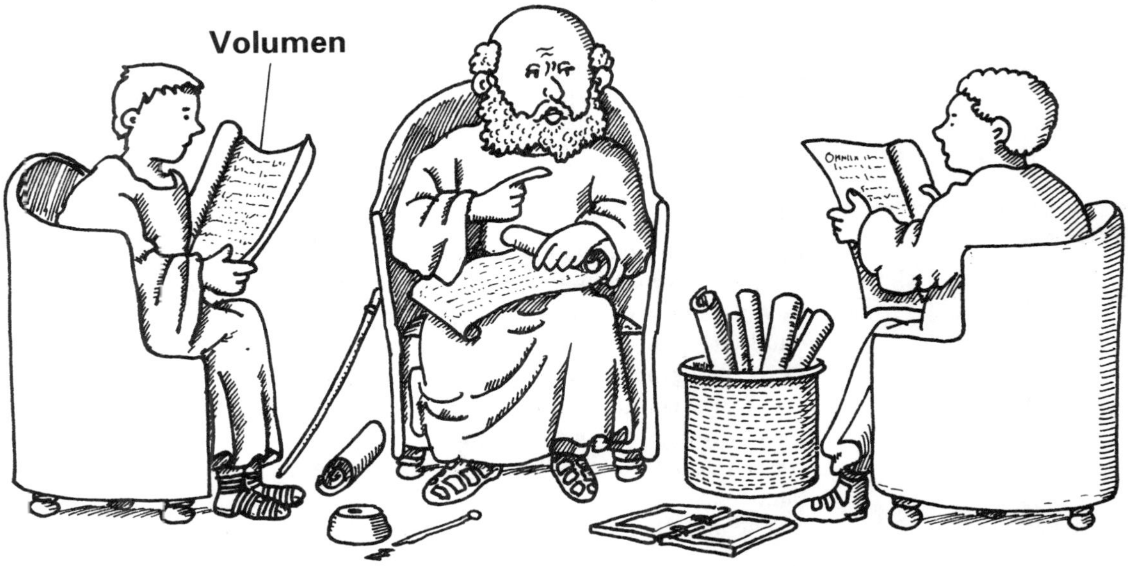

Volumen

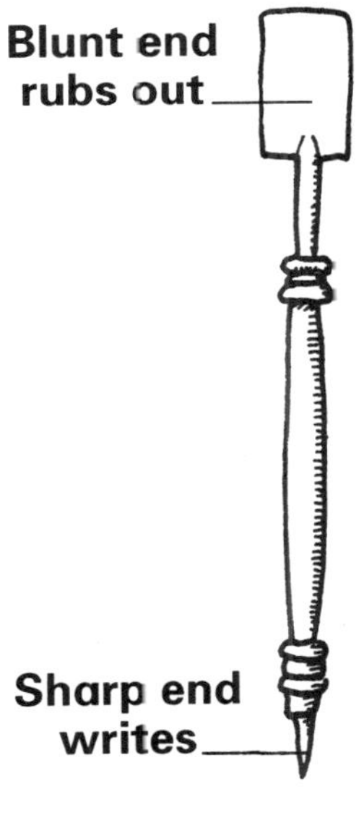

**Blunt end
rubs out**

**Sharp end
writes**

Stilus

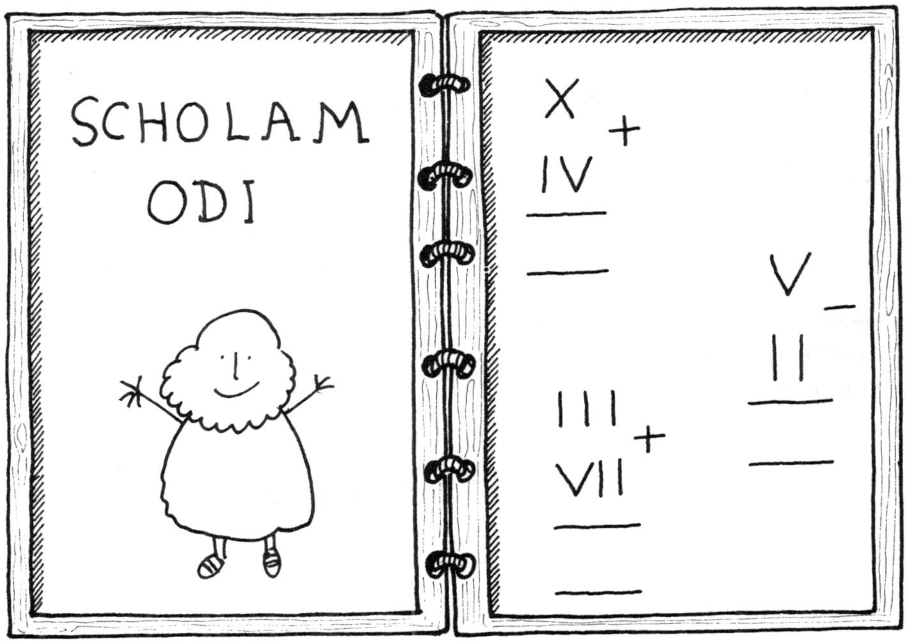

SCHOLAM
ODI

X +
IV
—

III +
VII
—

V —
II
—

Tabula

When they were learning to write, Romans used a wooden
board covered in wax. They scratched letters into this with a
stylus. This way they could easily rub out any mistakes.

Romans spoke and wrote in a language called Latin. Use
the Latin dictionary to work out what Valerius has written
on his wax board and the answers to his sums.

11 The temple

Skills

Using historical evidence
Making deductions from historical evidence
Being aware of more than one interpretation of the past

Attainment targets

Level	AT 1	AT 2	AT 3
2			
3			
4		↓	↓
5			

Introductory work

The two lead tablets shown on the activity sheet tell a story about a lost pig from different points of view, that of the owner of the pig and that of the person who now possesses it. This idea of an event being interpreted in two completely different ways like this could be explained to the children by discussing two children's accounts of something that happened in the playground. Although both accounts give details about the same event they could be different. Why do they think that is? As an introductory activity the teacher could give the children two or more written accounts of an incident and ask them to say what they think really happened.

The activity sheet also gives information about the nature of Roman temples and religion, and how people used them. 'Making a sacrifice' may need some preliminary explanation; in Roman sacrifices only animals were killed, not humans. (See also *Religion* (16).)

Using the sheet

Pick and Shovel appear again to reinforce the idea of finding and interpreting evidence. Their presence may help to emphasise that we found out about Roman religion from archaeological remains such as the lead tablets.

The second activity requires the children to look carefully at the characters visiting the priest to work out what they will be asking for.

Extension activities

1 Children could make up their wishes to be 'carved' on 'lead tablets'. They could make the tablets out of clay and scratch on their messages with a pencil or stick.
2 Children could choose one of the characters shown visiting the priest in the lower picture and write a story about why this character has come to the temple, as if they were that person.

The Romans worshipped many gods and goddesses. Each god had his or her own temple.

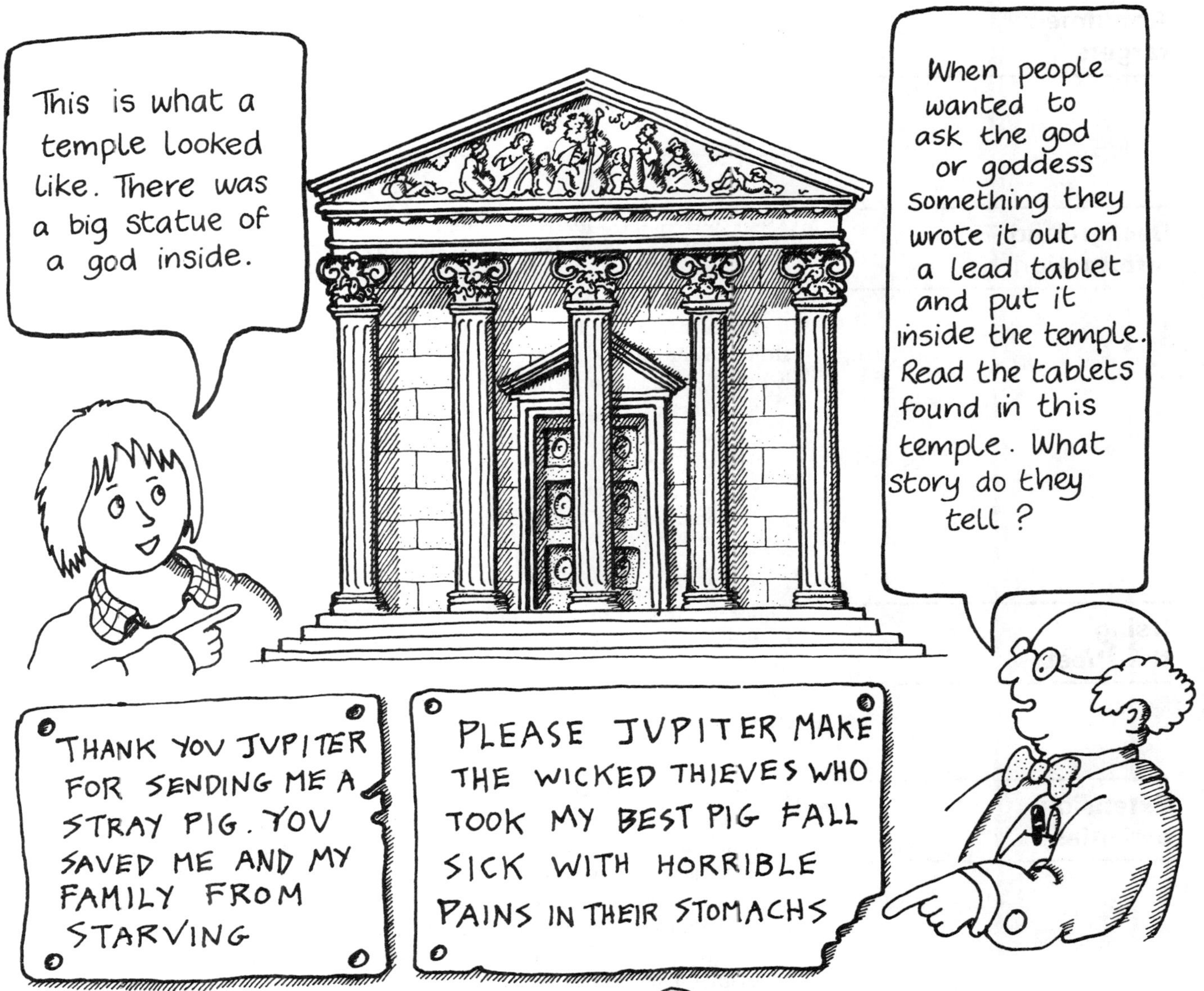

This is what a temple looked like. There was a big statue of a god inside.

When people wanted to ask the god or goddess something they wrote it out on a lead tablet and put it inside the temple. Read the tablets found in this temple. What story do they tell?

THANK YOU JUPITER FOR SENDING ME A STRAY PIG. YOU SAVED ME AND MY FAMILY FROM STARVING

PLEASE JUPITER MAKE THE WICKED THIEVES WHO TOOK MY BEST PIG FALL SICK WITH HORRIBLE PAINS IN THEIR STOMACHS

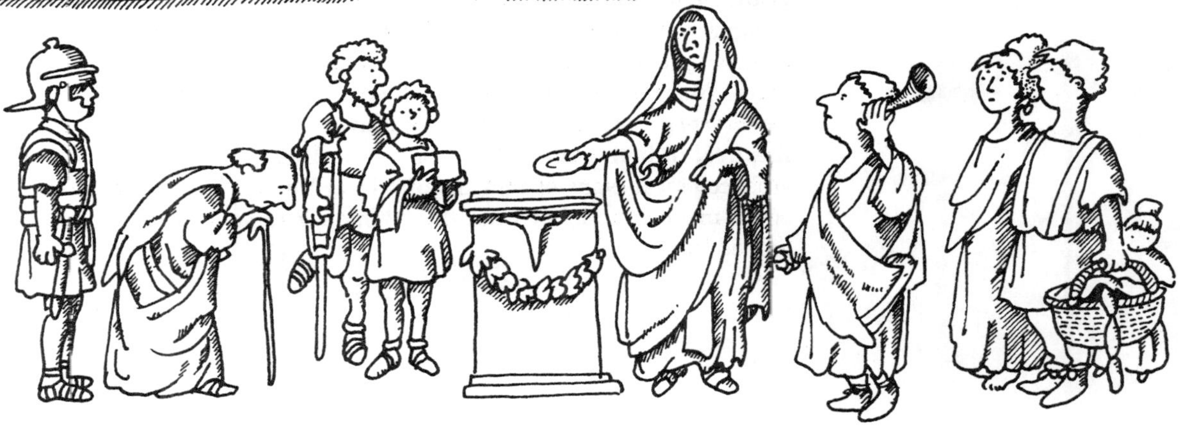

This picture shows a priest making a sacrifice outside the temple. Why do you think each of these people is visiting the priest?

12 Entertainment and the amphitheatre Teacher's notes

Skills

Using historical evidence
Making deductions from evidence

Attainment targets

Level	AT 1	AT 2	AT 3
2			↓
3			
4			
5			

Background information

The evidence that tells us gladiator fights took place are written accounts of the time and the archaeological remains of amphitheatres. Later on, Christians were cruelly killed and the children may know the Bible story of Daniel and the lion.

Amphitheatres looked very similar to modern football/athletic stadiums, although the 'sports' performed there were obviously very different! This is how Seneca, a Roman historian, described one of the shows:

'In the morning, men are thrown to the lions and bears; at lunchtime they're thrown to the spectators who demand that the man who has just killed his opponent should face the next man who will kill him in turn . . . and when the show stops for an intermission, the crowd cry: "Come on! Let's have some action – let's see some throats being slit." '

Using the sheet

Children should use the information in the drawings on the activity sheet to design a poster advertising a show. The poster should encourage people to come to the show, so the children will need to consider what the Romans would want to see – the more bloodthirsty the better, if Seneca is anything to go by!

Extension activities

1 Gladiator fights were not the only form of entertainment open to the Romans. They also enjoyed plays and comedies, poetry readings, music and chariot races. Children could make a table comparing entertainment in a Roman town with the facilities on offer in their own towns. They could produce entertainment guides for each.
2 The children could look at each of the gladiators and describe the different sorts of clothes and weapons. If the children had to be a gladiator which one would they choose to be?
3 Imagine you are a spectator at the games. Describe an afternoon's entertainment, including the sights, sounds, smells, etc.
4 David Macaulay's book *City – A Story of Roman Planning and Construction* contains excellent ink drawings of amphitheatres and theatres, in both plan and section views. Using the drawings and/or archaeological plans of remains of a local Roman theatre, children could make a model of what they think a Roman theatre/amphitheatre looked like.

Entertainment and the amphitheatre

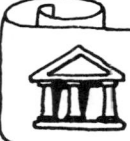

Larger towns in Roman Britain had theatres where plays were put on. Some towns had amphitheatres where other entertainments took place.

The Romans had a cruel sense of fun. They liked to see animals and people fighting each other. The men who fought each other were called gladiators.

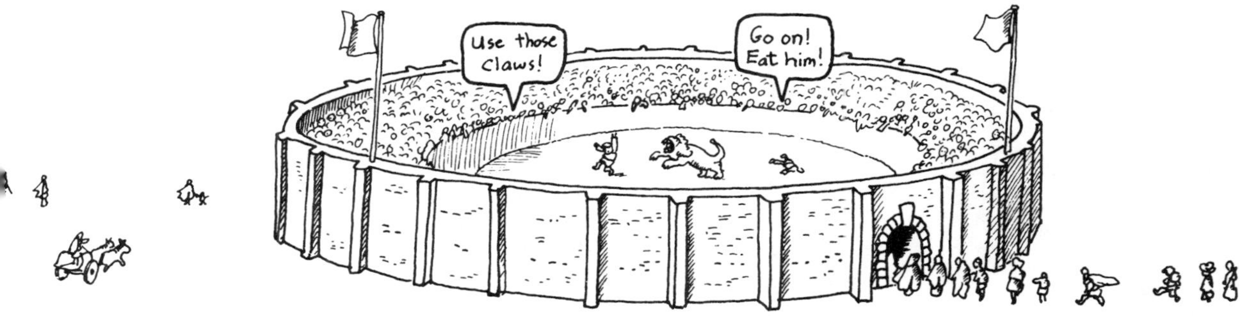

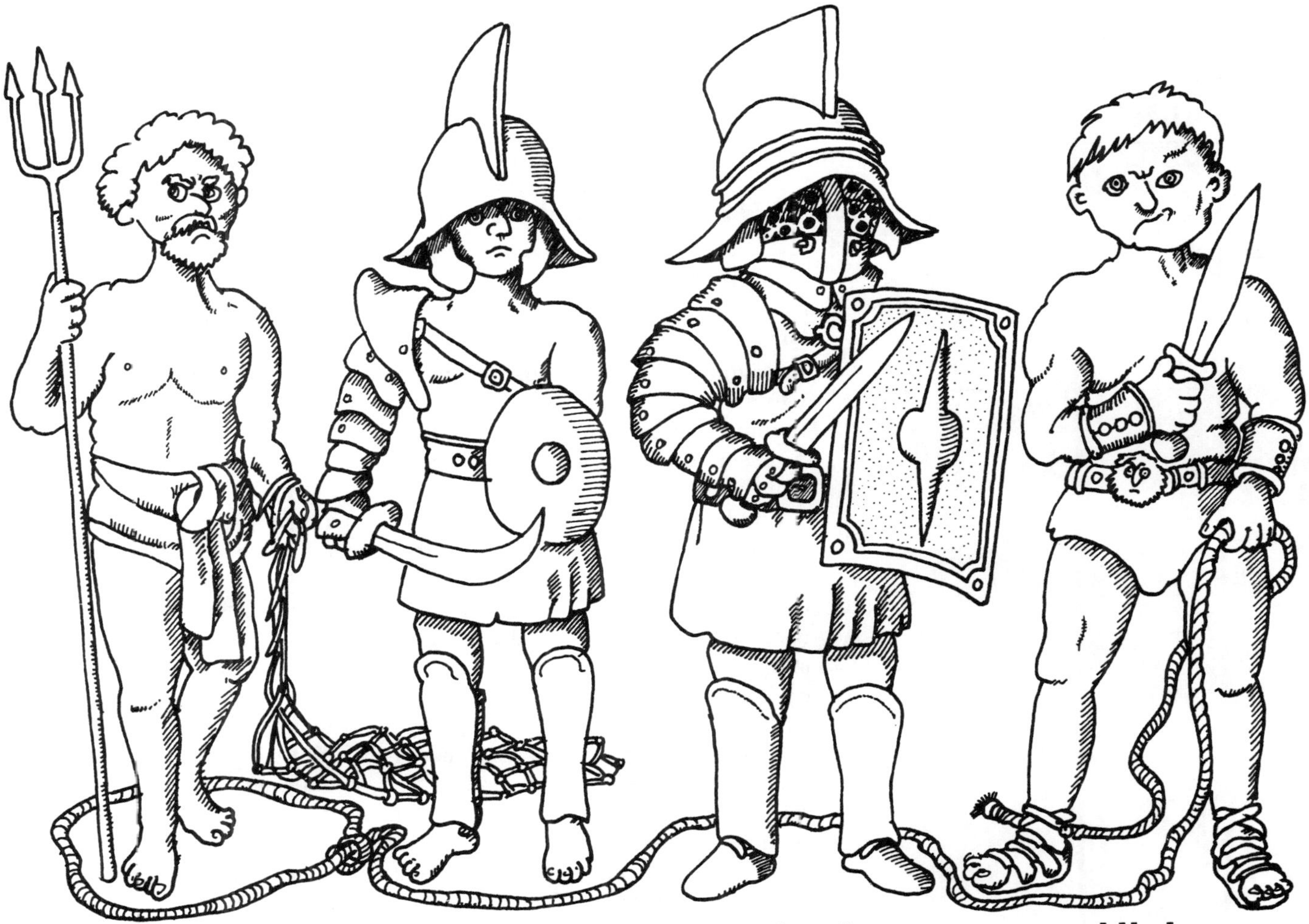

Didius **Glaucus** **Lucius** **Ulpius**

Design a poster advertising a show with two fights, using the gladiators in the picture. What could you put on the poster to make people want to come to the show?

13 The Roman town

Skills

Using historical evidence
Making deductions from evidence
Sequencing events

Attainment targets

Level	AT 1	AT 2	AT 3
2			↓
3			
4			
5			

Background information

Most Roman towns were laid out by army surveyors and engineers. Hence they often strongly resembled army camps/forts. Indeed, many towns in Roman Britain were originally army camps/forts which grew and developed into towns. The main features of Roman towns are town walls, gates on the north, south, east and west sides, main streets running north–south and east–west, a grid-like layout and often a ditch running outside the walls. Not many people would live within the city walls and often some of the buildings, e.g. the amphitheatre, would be outside.

Using the sheet

Before starting this sheet it might be useful if children have looked at previous sheets 7, 8, 9, 11 and 12 which all give information about particular buildings in the Roman town. The children should be able to work out the order in which Simplicius visits each building by using the clock faces. They should then present his visit in the form of a diary. The diary could be illustrated with each day presented as a series of pictures or as a strip cartoon.

Extension activities

1 Children could research Roman town names (see also *Place names* (20)). This list gives some of the main towns with their Roman names: Londinium – London; Deva – Chester; Glevum – Gloucester; Verulamium – St Albans; Lindum – Lincoln; Ratae – Leicester; Corinium – Cirencester; Aquae Sulis – Bath; Eburacum – York; Viroconium – Wroxeter; Isca – Exeter; Calleva – Silchester; Durovernum – Canterbury.

 Children could plot the Roman towns on a map of Britain and research roads and routes between the towns. (See also *Roads and trade* (14).)

2 Children could consider why they think defence of towns was necessary. They could list the defensive features of the town and give each one marks out of 10 according to how effective they might be, e.g. high city walls – 9 out of 10. How would they improve the existing features and what might they build to make the town really safe? Draw a new plan showing these new defences.

3 Children could make a town guide. They could even do a tape recording of a conducted tour around a Roman town. (This would be particularly good if you have a local site.)

4 Compare the plan of the town on the activity sheet with a plan of the children's own town. What similarities and differences can they spot?

The Roman town

This is a bird's-eye view of a Roman town in Britain. Simplicius, an old friend of Julius Maximus, has just visited the town. The clocks show when he visited each building. Work out in which order he visited buildings A to E. Plot his journey through the town starting at the South Gate in the afternoon.

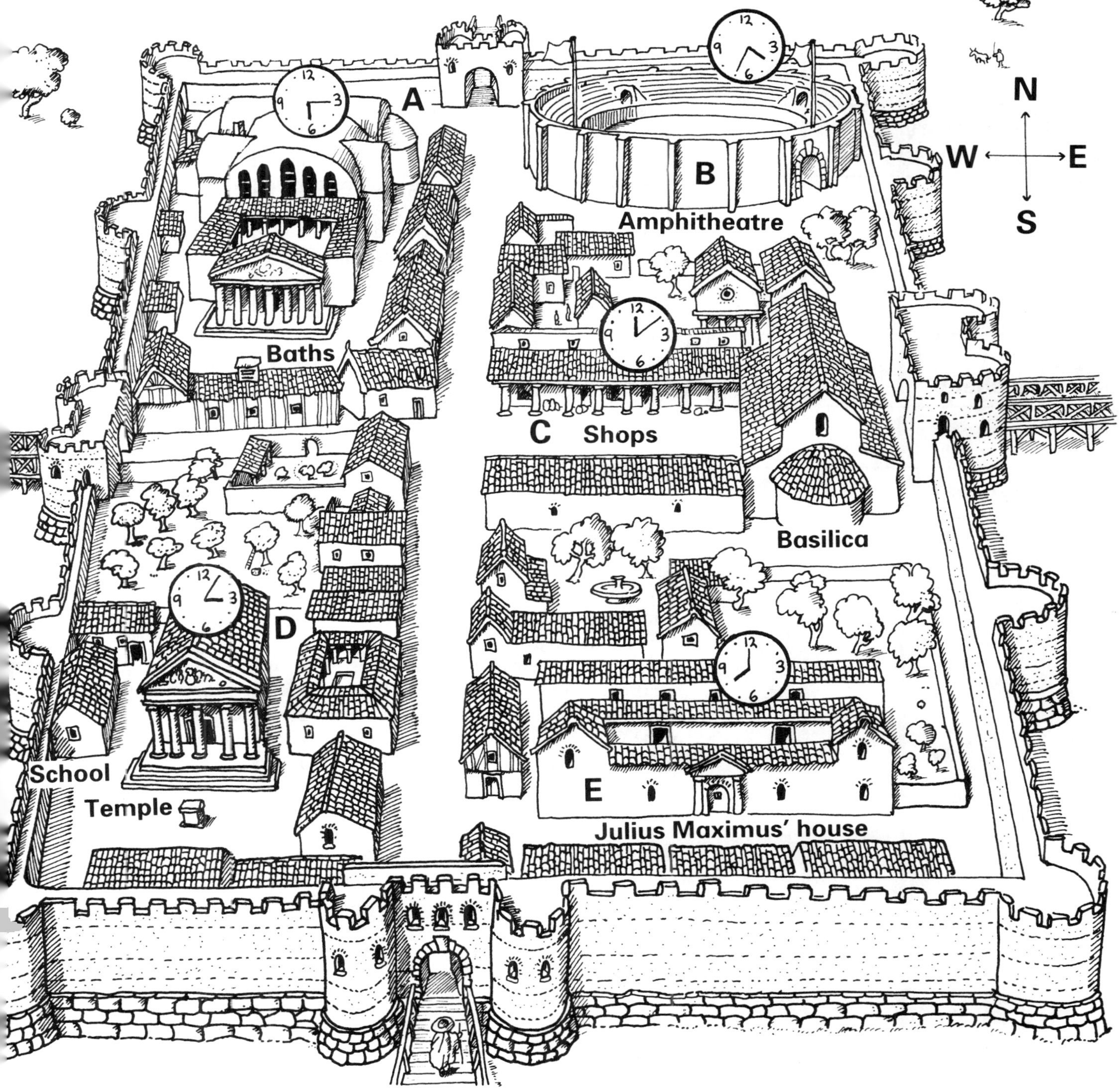

A

B
Amphitheatre

N
W ← → E
S

Baths

C Shops

Basilica

D

School

Temple

E

Julius Maximus' house

Write a diary of the day as if you are Simplicius. Give details of what you think he would have done in each building.

14 Roads and trade

Skills

Using historical evidence
Making deductions from evidence
Using historical language

Attainment targets

Level	AT 1	AT 2	AT 3
2			
3			↓
4			
5			

Introductory work

Teachers may wish to do some preliminary work on how Roman towns were linked by roads before doing this sheet.

As an introductory activity, the children could identify where each of the objects on the sheet comes from and plot those places on a map of the Roman Empire with a picture key.

Trade was a vital part of the Roman Empire. The class could discuss why goods were imported and exported, possibly linking this with trading today between European countries.

Using the sheet

The delivery slips could be written on card, made out as labels, or the information presented in table form. They could make an exhibition of the goods, using cardboard cut-outs with labels attached and maps to show where the goods have come from and where they are going.

Extension activities

1 Children could talk about what the different goods are and what they might have been used for. For example, why might Flavia want purple dye?

2 Children could research the extent of the Roman Empire. They could plot the route the ship might have taken to pick up each of the objects. If the ship started at the Roman port of Brindisi (southern Italy) what would be the most convenient route to pick the objects up and deliver them to the English port of Dover?

3 Children could research Roman roads. Many of the books listed in the resources section at the front of the book will have information about roads. Why were they built? Where were they built? How were they built? Can the children work out how the Romans might have made their roads straight? Do they know of any modern instruments for ensuring straight lines?

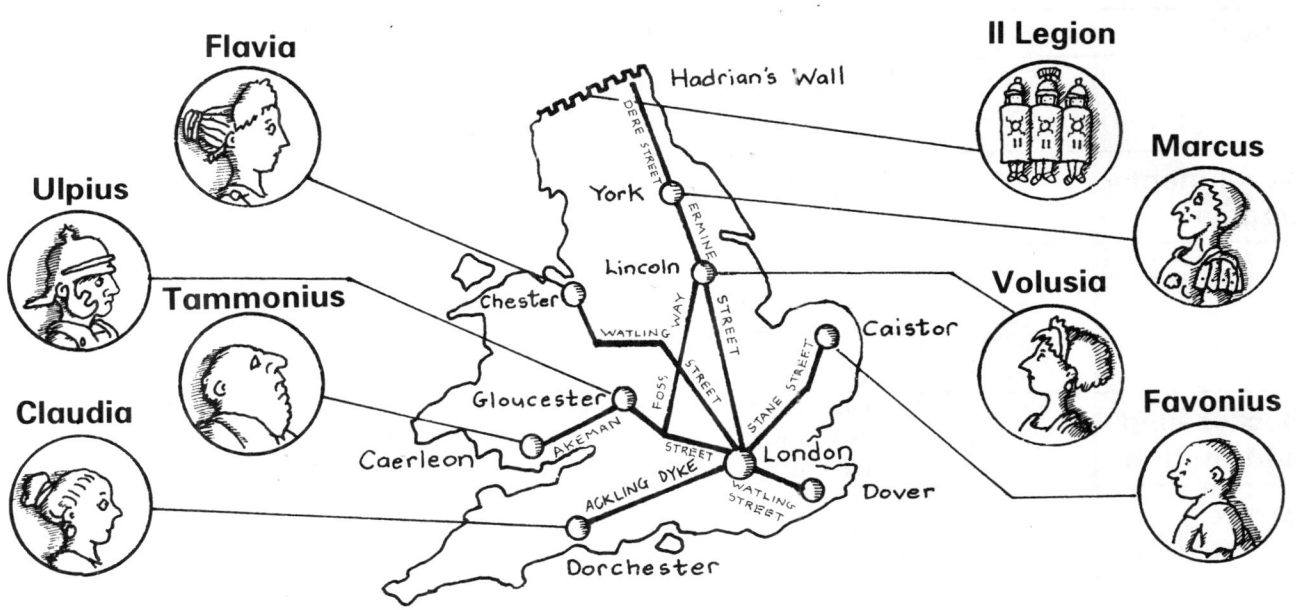

The Romans built long straight roads between all their towns.
How do you think this helped soldiers and traders?

Samian pottery (Gaul) — TO Ulpius, TO Ulpius

Spices (Syria) — TO Tammonius

Purple dye (Egypt) — TO Flavia

Wine (Italy) — TO II Legion

Silver (Italy) — TO Claudia

Letters (Rome) — TO Marcus

Glassware (Greece) — TO Volusia

Olive oil (Spain) — TO Favonius

Goods from far away places were brought to Britain by ship. These
goods have arrived at Dover. Make delivery slips like this for each item.

To	At	Via
Volusia	Lincoln	Watling Street, London and Ermine Street

15 The Roman villa

Skills

Using historical evidence
Making deductions from evidence
Reconstruction of the past from evidence

Attainment targets

Level	AT 1	AT 2	AT 3
2			↓
3			
4			
5			

Background information

One of the main points to make about Roman villas is that only very rich people would have lived in them. There is very little evidence left of the huts that the majority of Britons would have lived in. There are archaeological remains of many villas around the country and they give us valuable clues about the way of life in Roman Britain.

Villas were often richly decorated with wall paintings and mosaic floors. They had central heating systems and flushable toilets. A family living in a villa, like that of Simplicius Simplex, would have had lots of slaves.

Using the sheet

Children will need a copy of Resource sheet 2 from which they should cut out the object cards, possibly mounting them onto card. The task is to match each object to the place in the villa where they think it might have been kept. The answers are:

Bronze statuette of Bacchus, god of wine (temple)
A Roman game with die and shaker (living room)
Bronze strigil, used for scraping oils off the body (baths)
Stone pestle and mortar (kitchen)
Ivory or bone comb (bedroom)
Iron sickle (barn and granary)
Iron sheep shears (barn and granary)
Glass jug and goblet (dining room)
Iron animal bit (stable).

The children could ask themselves the following questions about each object: What do they think it is? What would it have been used for? How big would it have been? What is it made of and how might it have been made? Is there a modern object like it that we use today?.

Extension activities

1 Children could make a guide book or tape a 'conducted tour' around Simplicius' villa. They would need to consider possible stopping points of interest and decide what information they want to say about each place.
2 Children could write an estate agent's blurb for Simplicius' villa. They would need to look at examples of modern adverts and consider what sort of information they should include about the villa.
3 Children could make mosaics out of painted egg shells, clay or paper. They will need to do some research beforehand to look at designs, patterns, etc. Fishbourne Roman palace, Verulanium museum or Chedworth Villa will send information/postcards of mosaics found at these sites. (Addresses and telephone numbers for these are in the resources section at the front of the book.)

 # The Roman villa

Temple

Dining room

Living room

Kitchen

Bedrooms

Hypocaust furnace

Bath house

Barn and granary

Stable

This is my country house – the villa of Simplicius Simplex.

Cut up and match the object cards to the places where you think they would have been kept in the villa.

16 Religion

Skills

Identifying differences between historical periods
Describing changes over a period of time

Attainment targets

Level	AT 1	AT 2	AT 3
2			
3	↓		
4			
5			

Background information

The changes in religion from Roman gods, through Saxon to the arrival of Christianity were not neat or total. Pockets of Christianity existed in Britain as early as AD 200 as a result of the spread of the new religion from the continent. However, the official religion was still the worship of the old Roman gods and the Emperor himself who was considered a god. In these early days of Christianity, Christians were cruelly treated and often put to death in the amphitheatre using wild animals. (See *Entertainment and the amphitheatre* (12).)

By AD 391 worship of the old gods had been banned and Christianity became the official religion. The Saxons introduced a new set of gods when they invaded Britain but Christianity was brought back by two groups of people, those led by St Columba from Ireland and a group from Rome led by St Augustine.

Using the sheet

The children should look for pictorial clues on the statues to help them work out the names of the gods. They might wish to redraw the statues and even make up some of their own. In order to work out which days of the week are named after particular gods they should look at the first letters of each god's name. Tuesday is Tiu (god of battle), Wednesday is Wodin (chief Saxon god), Thursday is Thor (god of thunder), Friday is Frigg (goddess of farming) and Saturday is Saturn (god of farming).

Extension activities

1   Children could make Plasticine or clay models of the Roman and/or Saxon gods.
2   Some of the months of the year were also named after gods and leaders of the invaders. You could give the children a list of the months and a list of the gods and see if they can match them up.
      January – Janus (Roman god of openings/beginnings)
      February – Februus (Roman god of cleanliness)
      March – Mars (Roman god of war)
      April – Aperire (Latin word meaning 'to open')
      May – Maia (Roman god, mother of Hermes)
      June – Juno (wife of Jupiter, ruler of the gods)
      July – Julius Caesar
      August – Emperor Augustus
      September, October, November, December – '7th', '8th', '9th' and '10th' months (the Roman calendar began in March).
3   Children could find out more about the early Christian saints, e.g. St Patrick, St Columba, St Aidan, St Augustine, and plot their journeys on a map.

Religion

The Romans worshipped many gods and goddesses. They put up statues of them in their temples. Help Marcus the mason fill in the names of the gods in these statues.

VENUS
GODDESS OF L ---

MARS
GOD OF W--

JUPITER
GOD OF G_D_

DIANA
GODDESS OF H--T--G

SATURN
GOD OF F-R---G

In about AD 200 more people became Christians. Christians worship one God. The Roman gods were forgotten.

When the Saxons invaded Britain they brought their own gods and Christianity almost died out. These pictures show some Saxon gods.

Wodin   **Frigg**   **Thor**   **Tiu**

But after about AD 500, monks arrived to convert the Saxons. After 200 years they were all Christians.

St COLUMBA

From

Ireland

St AUGUSTINE

From

Rome

Look at the gods on this page to see which ones gave their names to the days of the week. Copy and fill in this calendar:

Day	Sunday	Monday	Tuesday	Wednesday	Thursday	Friday	Saturday
God	Sun	Moon					

17 The Saxons

Skills

Using historical evidence
Reconstructing the past from evidence
Making deductions from evidence
Evaluating evidence

Attainment targets

Level	AT 1	AT 2	AT 3
2			↓
3			
4			
5			↓

Background information

You may wish to set this sheet on the Saxons in an historical context before presenting it to the children. The historical outline in the introduction gives further information about the arrival and settlement of the Saxons. You should also give them some information about Alfred, King of Wessex, to cover National Curriculum requirements. One thing the children might pick up on straight away is how different the settlement is to the sophisticated Roman towns. The children could perhaps suggest reasons for this change (e.g. the Saxons were farmers, not town dwellers).

Using the sheet

This sheet shows the different sorts of evidence archaeologists might discover when excavating a Saxon settlement. The children are asked to act as historians and examine the clues to form their own picture of what Saxon life was like. They might like to present their own archaeological report, or they could draw their own impression of a Saxon settlement (you could blank out the picture at the top of the sheet before photocopying so it doesn't influence the children's ideas if you choose this option).

The objects found are:
A. A spear/arrow head. The bits of wood on the end should give them the clue that the object would have been attached to something wooden.
B. Clay weights used to weigh down the wool on a loom. The children will probably come up with something very inventive for this one!
C. Bone needle. Working out the size of this object using the scale should help them guess what it is.
D. Brooch. Again, working out the size and the materials from which this object is made will help them.

Extension activities

1 Ask children to make a list of the main differences between a Saxon hut and modern house today.
2 What factors do the children think would be important to Saxons choosing a village site? Nearness to a stream/river, nearness to wood supply? Ask them to design and plan a village showing the resources which made them choose that spot.
3 The story of Beowulf, written down in about the 8th century, gives lots of clues to the way of life of the Saxons. It would also be useful to consider how much we can trust this evidence – is it just a fairy tale or is it fact?
4 Children could make a model of a Saxon village using wood and straw. Each hut could be personalised by adding a Saxon family made or drawn by the children. This could extend into drama/rôle-play work, with children acting out Saxon family life.
5 Children could make a working Saxon loom, experiment with weaving, use vegetable dyes to colour cloth, make pottery bowls, cups, cooking pots, etc.

The Saxons

Thegn's hall

Churl's hut A

Churl's hut B

The Saxons lived in small villages. The main building was the hall of the chief called the Thegn. Churls were peasants who lived in huts built mainly of wood. These have now all disappeared. Archaeologists can sometimes reconstruct them using the evidence found when digging up a site.

It's no good. I'll never finish our report on the dig in time!

Perhaps you can help. We have found these remains of a Saxon house. This is all that is left of one of the houses in the picture above. Which one do you think it is? Draw the finds **A** to **D** and say what you think they are.

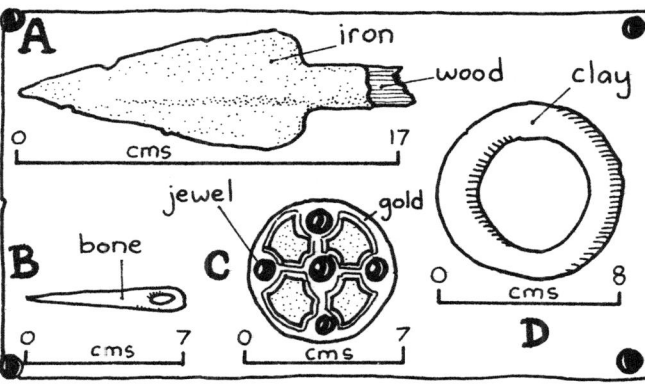

A iron wood clay
o cms 17

jewel gold
bone
B **C** **D**
o cms 7   o cms 7   o cms 8

plan of Saxon house
post holes
burnt ashes and stones

18 The Vikings

Teacher's notes

Skills

Using historical evidence
Making deductions from evidence

Attainment targets

Level	AT 1	AT 2	AT 3
2			↓
3			
4			
5			

Introductory work

Useful introductory work could be done on where the Vikings came from and children could find out the modern names for those places. Children could plot the routes by which the Vikings came to Britain, find out what methods of transport they used, where they landed and how they advanced into Saxon Britain. This could be done in a lively way, e.g. children could present it as a board adventure game or as a newspaper front page using background information from research books (see suggested booklists in the resources section at the front of this book).

Using the sheet

The carving of the Viking ship presents the children with some 'primary evidence' from which they can make deductions about the questions written underneath. These might be discussion pointers for small groups of children or answered individually in written form.

The Runic alphabet presents an alternative source of evidence and the children should have fun translating and writing their own messages. They could also invent their own names for other weapons and write these in Runes.

Extension activities

1 As well as giving their weapons names, Viking warriors also had nicknames, e.g. Ivarr the Boneless, Harold Bluetooth, Ulf the Unwashed – all intended to present a frightening and threatening character! Children could invent nicknames based on their own names and characteristics, e.g. Jason Redhair, Claire the Netball Player!
2 One group of children could write a newspaper report from the Saxon point of view ('The Daily Saxon') describing the Viking invasion, another group could write one from the Viking point of view ('The Viking Times'). This would be a good way of introducing 'bias' and the idea that people's interpretations of past conflicts depend on whose 'side' they were on.
3 The Bayeux Tapestry depicts the Norman invasion of Britain. Children could draw or present in collage form their own version of the tapestry representing scenes from the Viking invasion of Britain.

The Vikings

In AD 800 the Saxons began to be attacked by the Vikings who sailed in their long ships from Norway and Denmark. At first they came to destroy and steal but later they decided to settle in Britain.

This is a carving of a Viking ship. Look at it carefully. How was the ship steered? How many men could it carry? Why do you think it had a beast's head on the front?

Vikings were very fond of their weapons. This sword is called 'brainbiter'. Why do you think they called it that? The symbols on the sword are a spell written in Runes – the Viking alphabet.

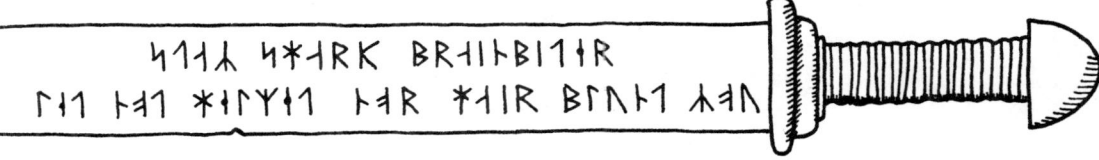

This is the Runic alphabet:

ᛏ ᛒ ᚤ ᚴ ᛁ ᛂ ᛃ ᚠ ᚥ ᚼ ᛁ ᛁ ᚴ ᚦ ᚤ ᚼ ᛂ ᚴ ᛘ ᚱ ᚾ ᛏ ᚢ ᚢ ᚿ ᚿ ᚾ ᛉ

A B Y C D E F G H I J K L M N O P Q R S T U V W X Y Z

Work out what the spell on the sword says. Try spelling your own name in Runes.

19 A changing town

Skills

Describing changes over a period of time
Identifying similarities and differences
Using historical evidence
Making deductions from evidence
Identifying different types of cause and consequence

Attainment targets

Level	AT 1	AT 2	AT 3
2			
3			↓
4			
5	↓		

Introductory work

This sheet can be used to draw together a lot of the different strands presented so far and put the whole period of 'invasions' in context. As an introductory activity you could present the children with maps of their own town, say, over the past three hundred years. Ask them to say how it has changed and developed.

Or they could do a similar activity over an even shorter time span, e.g. looking at how their school has changed over the past 20 years. They could make a wall display showing how changes in the aspect of the town or school has reflected changes in the way of life of, say, the last two generations. It is important that they look for similarities as well as differences.

Using the sheet

It would be useful for children to discuss the changes in the towns with a partner or in small groups. They could draw up a table in which to record their answers. The three pictures clearly show a backward development. Pointers for discussion include: Which of the three periods would they like to live in and why? What do they think were the reasons for the changes? What happened to the building materials used by the Romans? How do we know the Roman town looked as it did if it was all knocked down?

Extension activities

1   Children could draw what the town would look like today and could even try drawing a futuristic view of the town.
2   This sheet shows the changes that took place in town planning over the period AD 300 – AD 900. Children could take a different area, e.g. costume or transport, and examine the changes to this area which occurred within the 'invaders and settlers' period. They could do this in pictorial or written form or on a timeline.
3   What happened after the Viking invasion? Was this the last invasion of Britain? Ask the children to find out if there were any invaders of Britain after the Vikings.

A changing town

AD 300
The Roman town

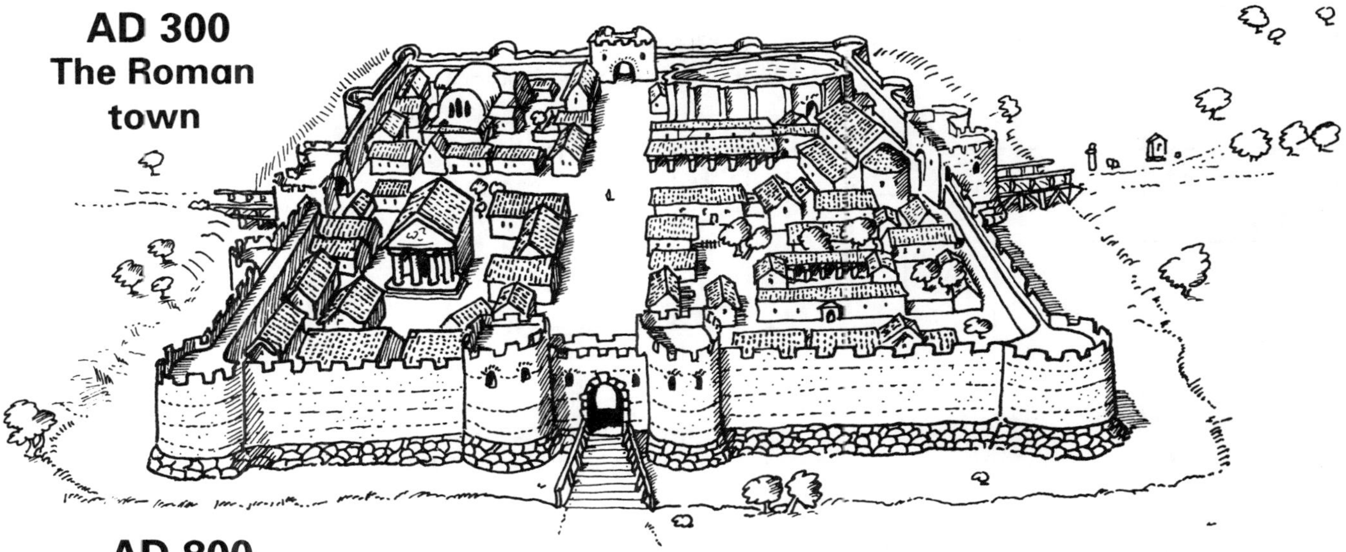

AD 800
After the Saxon invasion

AD 900
After the Vikings settle

Look at these three pictures. They show how towns changed from Roman to Viking times.

What are the differences between the three towns? What has changed and what has stayed the same?

20 Place names

Skills

Using historical evidence
Using historical language
Identifying differences between historical periods

Attainment targets

Level	AT 1	AT 2	AT 3
2			
3	↓		↓
4	↓		
5			

Background information

Maps and place names are an excellent form of evidence and even if the town the children live in doesn't go back to Roman, Saxon or Viking times there will be somewhere nearby that does.

Your local records office, archives or local history society should be able to provide copies of, or at least access to, old maps, drawings or photographs, parish records, etc., which would be very useful.

Using the sheet

Pick and Shovel make a final appearance to emphasise that place names and maps are a form of evidence. Children should read through the table carefully before doing the colouring exercise.

The pattern produced by underlining the place names clearly shows that the Viking names are restricted to the East coast and mid/north England. Apart from that, the towns of Roman and Saxon origin are well-mixed and show that Saxon settlers reached far into Britain rather than just keeping to the coast.

Extension activities

1 On a map of their local area children could do a similar colouring exercise on nearby villages and towns. Can they find evidence of a fort or farm in these places that might go back to Roman, Saxon or Viking times?
2 Children could investigate the origins of names other than those on the sheet. For example, surnames give clues to their origins, either occupational or geographical; school names or house names; street names give clues to the past history of the town, e.g. there is often a 'Station Road' even after the railway has disappeared; town names apart from those with Roman, Saxon and Viking endings.
3 You could give the children the name and address of a person and ask what these tell them, e.g. 'John Cooper, The Old Bakery, Farm Close, Molesworth'.

Or they could make up their own names and/or research to find 'real' examples in the local area.

Place names

We can often tell where the Romans, Saxons and Vikings lived from the names of their towns and villages.

The ending of each place name tells us whether it was a Roman, Saxon or Viking town or village.

People	Endings of place names	What they mean	Example
Roman	Chester Caster Caistor	castrum = a fort	Dorchester Tadcaster Caister-on-Sea
Saxon	borough burgh bury ing ham ton wich	burh = a fort ingas = the place of ham = village tun = farmstead wic = farm	Loughborough Edinburgh Canterbury Seething Sheringham Kidlington Ipswich
Viking	by thorpe toft	by = farmstead or village torp = farm toft = homestead	Wragby Grimthorpe West Tofts

Look at the map. Underline Roman town names in red, Saxon names in blue and Viking names in green.

Resource Sheet 1

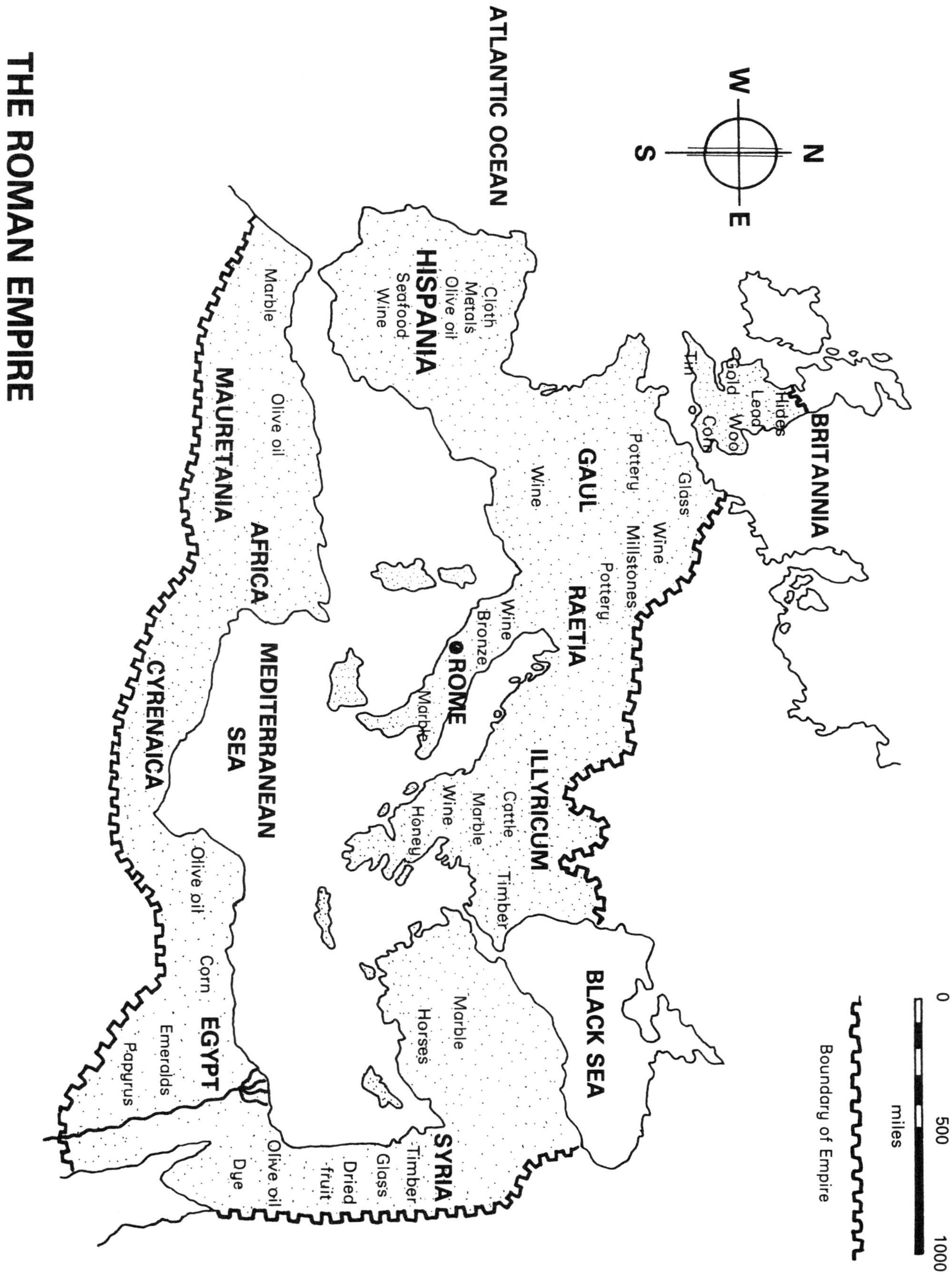

THE ROMAN EMPIRE

ATLANTIC OCEAN

W · N · E · S

HISPANIA
Cloth
Metals
Olive oil
Seafood
Wine

BRITANNIA
Tin
Gold
Lead
Wool
Corn
Hides

GAUL
Wine
Pottery
Wine
Millstones
Glass
Pottery

RAETIA

MAURETANIA
Marble

AFRICA
Olive oil

CYRENAICA

MEDITERRANEAN SEA
Olive oil

● ROME
Wine
Bronze
Marble

ILLYRICUM
Wine
Cattle
Marble
Timber
Honey

BLACK SEA
Marble
Horses

EGYPT
Corn
Emeralds
Papyrus

SYRIA
Olive oil
Dye
Dried fruit
Glass
Timber

0 — 500 — 1000
miles

Boundary of Empire

Resource Sheet 2

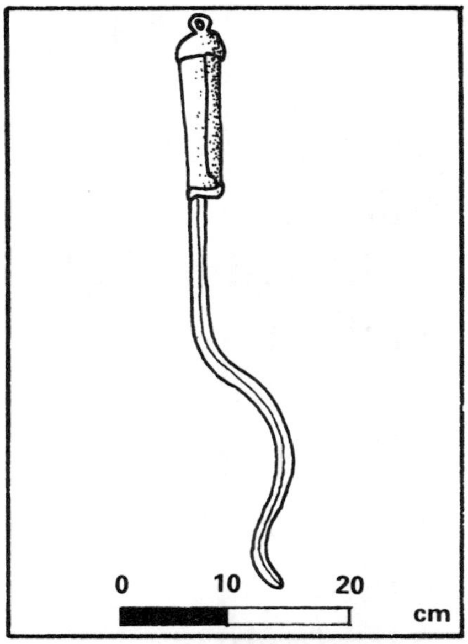

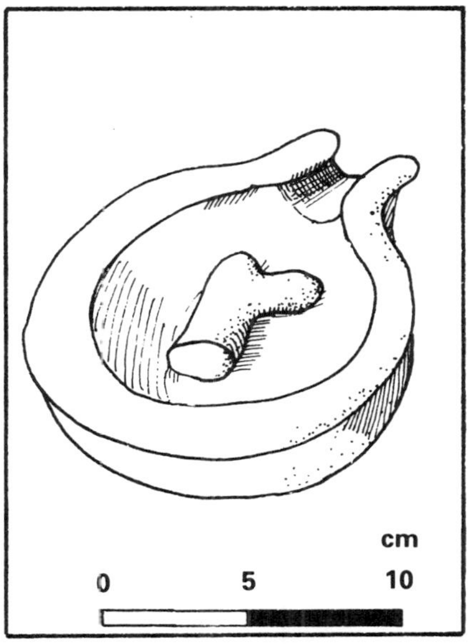

cm
0   100
BACHVS

0   10   20
cm

0   10   20
cm

cm
0   5   10

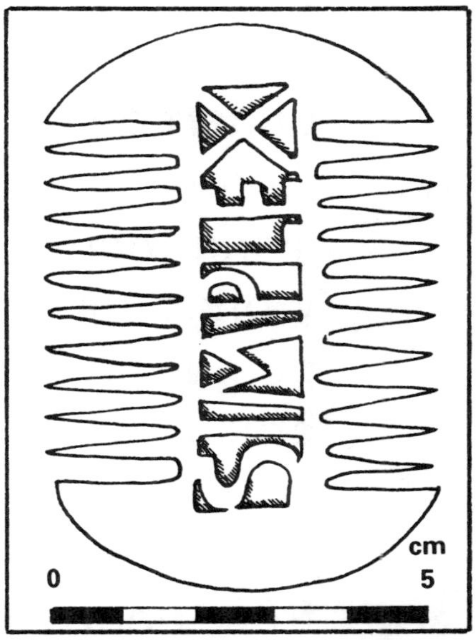

SIMPLEX
cm
0   5

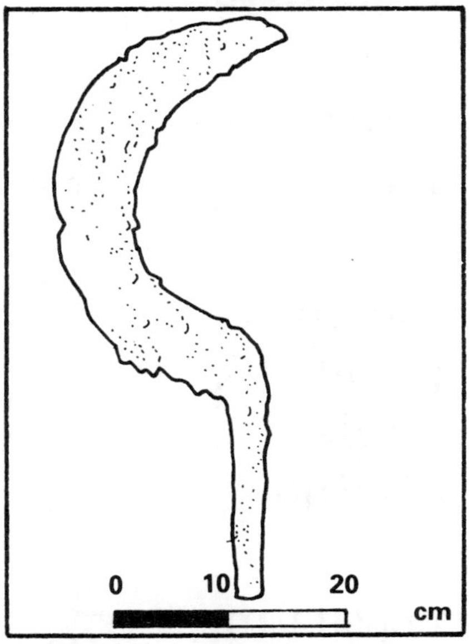

0   10   20
cm

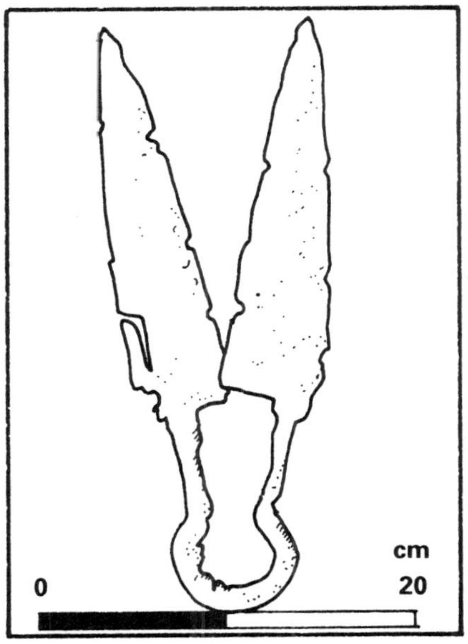

cm
0   20

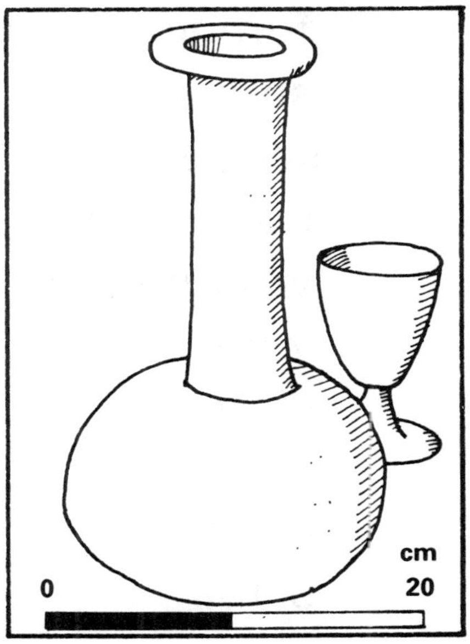

cm
0   20

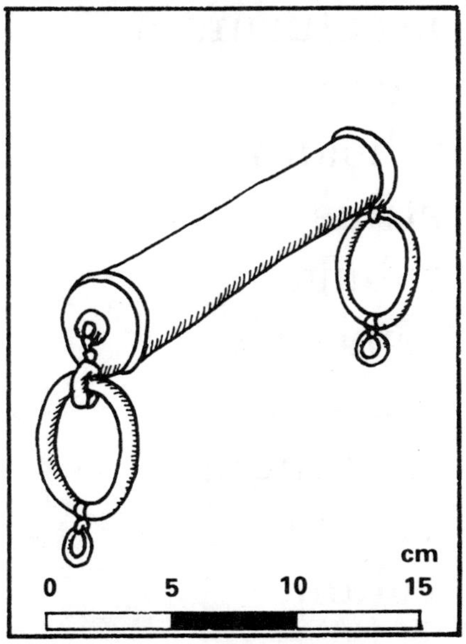

cm
0   5   10   15

© Fiona Goodman and Peter Kent. Simon & Schuster Education. 1991.

Latin dictionary

apodyterium	cloakroom
calceus	shoes
calidarium	hot room
calumus	pen
carnis	meat
cubiculum	bedroom
cubiculum servum	slave's room
culina	kitchen
frigidarium	cold room
holeris	vegetables
hypocaust	underfloor central heating system
odi	I hate
oecus	living room
officina	workroom
palaestra	gymnasium
panis	bread
piscina	pool
porticus	porch
posticum	front door
praefurnium	furnace room
sacrarium	shrine
scholam	school
stilus	pointed tool for writing on wax
tabula	wax writing board
tepidarium	warm room
textum	cloth
triclinium	dining room
vinum	wine
volumen	scroll